# MAGIC QUESTIONS

How to change your life at the speed of thought

## KEITH ELLIS

**Distribution**

This book is available from Ingram for distribution to libraries, bookstores, educational institutions, and wholesalers.

https://www.ingramcontent.com/

**Published by KeithEllis.com LLC**
Washington, DC

ISBN: 978-1-7350714-2-8 (Paperback)
ISBN: 978-1-7350714-0-4 (E-Book)

# Disclaimer

A *Magic Question*™ is powerful medicine. If you ask yourself any of the questions in this book, or follow any advice you may find here, you do so at your own risk.

If you choose to read beyond this page, you agree that:

1. Neither the Author nor the Publisher assumes any liability whatsoever for the Reader's actions, or consequences of the Reader's actions, whether or not those actions may be said to have been influenced by this book, or any other material referenced in this book.

2. Neither the Author nor the Publisher makes any warranty of any kind, expressed or implied, about the usefulness, practicality, or safety of anything written or referenced here.

If you're not willing to comply with these limitations, please do not read this book.

# About the Author

Keith Ellis is an inspirational speaker, a passionate photographer, and a bestselling author.

He reinvented the art and science of setting goals in his classic: **The Magic Lamp**: *Goal Setting for People Who Hate Setting Goals*, a book that's helped more than a hundred thousand people around the world in half a dozen languages.

He's also the author of the best-selling thriller, **No Secrets**. These works couldn't be more different. But whether you're a writer or a reader it's fun to use both sides of your brain.

He's created a website that offers a new *Magic Question* every week. There's no spam, no ads, and no charge. Just magic.

To learn more, visit:

### Weekly Magic™

### KeithEllis.com

**f** facebook.com/KeithEllisMagic

**𝕏** twitter.com/KeithEllisMagic

**in** linkedin.com/in/KeithEllisMagic

**◯** instagram.com/KeithEllisMagic

**𝕡** pinterest.com/KeithEllisMagic

# Acknowledgements

Special thanks to Alan Ellis, Helen English Guthrie, and Dr. Robert Guthrie for their invaluable comments and suggestions at various phases of this project.

*To Maggie, you fill my life with magic.*

# Table of Contents

## Part 3: Magic at Work

## Part 4: The Magic of People

## Prologue

*W*hen the World Wide Web began to reinvent the world, I joined an internet startup named webMethods. I was their fifth employee. As the newly minted vice president of sales my job was to sell a product that wasn't finished, from a company no one had heard of, to a market that didn't exist.

I struggled.

Within a few months we were running out of money. As a professional salesperson, I was in the business of asking other people questions, so I decided to ask myself one:

*How can I make us famous overnight?*

The answer appeared as if by magic. The easiest way to become known for what you do is to become associated with someone who is already known for what they do. Someone who can lend their reputation to yours.

As so often happens, one good question led to another:

*Who can help me do that?*

Again, like magic, the answer appeared. There was only one person in our embryonic industry who was already a rock star. His name was Tim Berners-Lee and he had invented the World Wide Web. He was the guy I needed to meet.

The problem was I didn't know him and I didn't know anyone who did. I would have googled him, but Google wasn't around yet. I could have tried to connect with him on Facebook or LinkedIn, but they didn't exist.

That raised an obvious question:

*How can I get in front of Tim Berners-Lee?*

More magic. It turned out he was scheduled to be the keynote speaker at an important trade conference in New York City only a few weeks hence. If I could make it there and somehow get his attention, then maybe I could convince him to help us.

Grasping at that straw, when the date arrived two of us headed to Manhattan.

We reached the show floor and set up our display. Leaving my colleague to handle the booth, I hustled to the keynote presentation where Berners-Lee was about to speak. My foolproof plan was to persuade the great man to come back to our booth with me. I just didn't have a clue how to do it.

The auditorium was humming with the anticipation of a crowd waiting for a celebrity to appear. But when Berners-Lee arrived and began to speak something was wrong. He must have had a terrible cold or the flu—maybe both—because he sounded awful. He kept pausing to hack and sneeze but he soldiered on.

When he finished, like any rock star he was mobbed by his fans, clamoring to meet the man whose technology was even then transforming the human experience. I stood on the periphery while his other admirers had their way with him. Every interaction seemed to drain a portion of what little energy he had left, but he never refused to shake a hand or respond to a question.

My turn came when everyone else had gone. I could tell Tim was exhausted. Yet to my everlasting shame, all I could think about was how to coax this weary soul to come with me so we could show him the technology we were developing. I still didn't know how I was going to do it.

Just shy of too late, a question flashed into my brain:

*What can I offer such an important person?*

I was already shaking his hand when the most magical question of all materialized:

*What if I could offer him a piece of our company?*

I had no authority to do that, of course, not without consulting our stockholders. Then again, what were the odds a man of his stature would say yes? As long as I was up front with him about it, I had nothing to lose.

On his last legs, Tim greeted me graciously, even kindly. I have no idea how he summoned the energy to do that, but I took a deep breath and launched into my thirty-second elevator pitch about the technology our engineers had invented.

His face lit up. "You're building a semantic network," he said, obviously delighted. "That's just what the web needs!"

I was stunned by such a positive reaction, but I plunged ahead and asked if he would be interested in joining our board of advisors in return for stock options, provided I could somehow persuade our stockholders to approve.

Tim smiled. "I'd be very interested," he said as we turned and walked toward our booth. "I may have helped create the web, but I've never made a penny from it."

Life has changed profoundly since then, thanks in large part to what Tim invented. Five billion people now use the World Wide Web in one form or another. Religion doesn't spread that fast. Tim is no longer just a rock star; he's a legend. He's not even Tim anymore. He is Sir Timothy John Berners-Lee, knighted by Queen Elizabeth of Great Britain because he changed the world. In a recent list of eighty cultural moments that shaped history, a panel of eminent thinkers ranked the invention of the World Wide Web as the most important of them all.[1]

Three years after that trade conference webMethods went public as the largest software IPO in history. Sir Timothy finally received some long-overdue compensation for the amazing gift he had bestowed upon the world. And I learned something I'll never forget:

*The questions we ask ourselves are magic.*

# Book I: THE MAGIC OF CHANGE

# 1

# What is a Magic Question?

*T*he simplest question can hijack your thoughts:

*What color are your mother's eyes?*

The wrong question can hijack your life.

Have you ever wondered what happens in the human brain when we ask a question? Even brain scientists don't know. There's evidence that being asked certain types of questions can increase activity in the parts of the brain where we experience pleasure and reward.[1] That doesn't tell us why it happens or what it means; all we know is it feels good.

There's also evidence that people change their behavior merely from being asked a question about it. In one study, when a group of people were asked if they intended to vote, 25% more of them voted than those in the control group, who hadn't been asked.[2] Another study found that when people in one group were asked if they were going to buy a car, they were 35% more likely to buy a car than were those in a group where no one was asked.[3] These are significant impacts just from being asked a question, but they still don't give us a clue about what's happening inside the brain, or why.

Human beings are a question-based life form. When we're asked a question, it creates a vacuum in our mind. Nature abhors a vacuum, so we have trouble thinking about anything else until we come up with an answer or are asked another question, which yanks our brain in a new direction. If science can't tell us why any of this happens, let me suggest an entirely unscientific explanation: Questions are magic. If that's too cosmic for you, how about this: *some questions feel like magic.*

What makes them so different from the rest?

A *Magic Question* isn't what you ask someone else, it's a question you ask yourself. That's where the magic begins.

There's nothing complicated about asking yourself a *Magic Question*. There's no ten-step process to memorize, no mantra to chant, no checklist to follow. The power of a *Magic Question* isn't limited by language, gender, culture, race, education, age, or IQ. Anyone on the planet can ask a *Magic Question* to help solve any problem.

*Magic Questions* let you hack into your brain to access mental resources that lie beneath the surface. Combine that with their uncanny power to cut through emotional red tape and *Magic Questions* become the ultimate catalyst for change.

When you ask yourself the right question at the right time, you change your life at the speed of thought.

But there's a trick to it. The right questions can take you wherever you want to go in life. The wrong questions take you in the opposite direction.

Never has this distinction been more important. As I write this, in the middle of the COVID-19 pandemic, sickness and death are beyond reckoning, the global economy has imploded, and the jobs of millions of people have simply vanished. The emotional shock of such a catastrophe is beyond words. Yet we struggle to find words anyway, often in the form of questions like these:

- *What will I do?*
- *How will I survive?*
- *How can I protect those I love?*
- *How can I pay my bills?*

- *How can I support my family?*
- *How can I cope with this?*
- *What happens next?*

It might be tempting to dismiss such questions as little more than expressions of despair, but that would be a mistake. They demonstrate how the mind tries to look for light at the end of even the longest, darkest tunnel.

Intention is what makes all the difference. When we ask questions like these to express our emotions, that's one thing. But when we ask the very same questions with the intent of exploring possibilities and solving problems, we make magic. We give ourselves the power to change our lives at the speed of thought.

## *Magic Principles*

The first principle of asking *Magic Questions* is to understand you have a choice. Like so many other things in our lives, the questions we ask ourselves often flow from habit. We tend to ask ourselves the same questions we've always asked and keep getting the same results. That's how we get stuck. But we don't have to remain that way. We can choose to ask ourselves different questions, becoming an active participant in our own life instead of a passive prisoner of old habits. We can choose to ask ourselves questions that take us where we want to go instead of where we've been.

The second principle is to realize you cannot escape making a choice. Either you choose to change the questions you ask yourself, or you choose not to. There are no alternatives. The choice begins and ends with you.

The third principle is that you can learn the habit of asking yourself the right question at the right time. In fact, you were born with it.

The process of asking and answering questions is how you became who you are. It started when you first began to think and talk. You asked questions about everything. As a child, your job description was to fill in the blanks. Through the years, as you began to piece together your model of the world, you had fewer blanks to fill in and asked fewer questions. Questions didn't disappear from your life, but they receded into the background.

What did disappear was the magic surrounding questions, the mystical sense of how the right question can summon the resources you need to meet life's challenges and opportunities. I've written this book to rekindle the magic. I want to reacquaint you with the power *Magic Questions* give you to shape your life—a power you grew up with. The same process that made you who you are can make you who you want to be.

Most of the questions in these pages will seem familiar. Don't worry about that. What makes a question magic is not whether you know it, but whether you use it, and how you use it. The only way to invoke this magic is to make the leap from merely reading a question to asking yourself that question and paying attention to your answers. The *Magic Worksheet*™ can help. You'll find it at the end of this book. Or download it here:

*www.keithellis.com/magic-worksheet*

What makes *Magic Questions* so powerful is that they're questions you ask yourself. The questions you ask other people may be important, but the questions you ask yourself can change your life. Like this one:

## What do I want from this book?

**Ask** yourself that question. **Listen** to the answers that form in your mind. **Capture** them on a piece of paper, or your favorite notes app, or on the palm of your hand. At this point, focus on quantity instead of quality. Write down everything your brain is trying to give you. When you're finished, give yourself a moment to ***reflect*** on what you've come up with. Together, these four magic words—ask, listen, capture, and reflect—will help you make the most of all the questions to come.

So will this:

How can I change my life at the speed of thought?

Keep this in the back of your mind as you're reading because it's the primary question this book will help you answer.

## *How to Read This*

You don't have to read this book from start to finish. In fact, you don't want to. If you try, you'll be overwhelmed. There are more than 400 questions here. Each is a tool to help you make a meaningful change in your life. Trying to change 400 things at once is a bit much for anyone to handle, so focus on one question at a time. Take as long as you need to extract as much value as you can from each question. Don't worry about the other 400; they'll be here when you need them.

Begin with *Book I: The Magic of Change*. It consists of twelve chapters, including this one, that set up everything that follows. Think of them as the main book. Together, they're only about fifty pages, but working through them will make you feel like you're earning a PhD in how to create the life you want. The questions in these chapters will challenge and stretch you in ways you can't yet imagine. More importantly, they'll teach you the habit of asking yourself questions that can change your life at the speed of thought. That's the best possible take away from reading this book.

Think of *Book II: Making Magic* as a reference book full of questions to ask yourself once you're comfortable asking yourself questions. When you're ready, you can get a lot out of *Book II* just by scanning the Table of Contents (or the Index of Magic Questions that points to every *Magic Question* in this book.) Each chapter is titled with a question. Each question is a portal: a door you can open to something new and exciting in your life. If a question catches your eye, follow wherever it takes you, as long as it takes you.

## *Give Yourself a Break*

When you're finished with *Book I*, congratulate yourself on earning that PhD and take a break from reading, but not from questions. Use the break to practice the habit of asking yourself *Magic Questions*.

When you come back from break, work through the chapters in *Book II* in any order you find useful. Take as much time as you need for the questions you encounter. Each is a golden opportunity to change your life at the speed of thought. Every one brings you a step closer to turning *Magic Questions* into a magic habit. When that happens, buckle your seatbelt.

Along the way, you may find that one good question leads to another. You may discover amazing new thoughts and insights. You may change your life in wonderful ways. You may even reach that light at the end of the tunnel.

If that's not magic, what is?

2

# What am I going to do about it?

*O*ur lives are the sum total of what happens to us and what we choose to do about it. Chance and choice are all we've got.

Unfortunately, there isn't much we can do about chance. No matter how loudly we protest the slings and arrows of outrageous fortune, it won't change a thing. That leaves us with choice. The only way we can make a difference in our lives is to choose to do so. Circumstances may limit our choices, often severely, but they don't eliminate them—and they don't spare us the requirement of choosing how we respond.

Psychologists have various opinions about when a human being reaches adulthood. I believe we become adults when we stop blaming the world for how we got here and take charge of where we want to go. We aren't responsible for anything beyond our control, but we are responsible for everything else. The questions you ask yourself will focus your attention on one or the other. It's your choice.

In a matter of weeks, COVID-19 upended our world. No one was untouched. No one escaped its effects. We will spend the rest of our lives in its wake.

In a crisis of that magnitude a feeling of helplessness can take over. It's a natural response to a new reality that feels out of control. But it's not the only response. Instead, you can ask this *Magic Question*:

## What am I going to do about it?

Place the emphasis on "I".

Asking this question will change your life. It won't change the world, at least not right off the bat, but it will change how you think about the world. That's how to change your life at the speed of thought. Shift your thinking into a different gear. Instead of focusing on what you can't control, focus on what you can. Choose how you respond.

Whatever the world throws at you, keep asking yourself that question above. Ask it when you feel helpless. Ask it when you have a problem to solve. Ask it when the world seems to be more than you can handle. Ask it when you can't think of anything else to do.

Listen to your answers. Capture them. Reflect on them. Use the *Magic Worksheet*.

Then do something about it. Every action you take will make you feel less helpless and more powerful in your own life.

As mere mortals, we don't get to choose what happens to us in life, but we can choose what we do about it. In that choice lies the difference between helplessness and hope.

### *Self-Pity*

A common byproduct of misfortune is to feel sorry for ourselves. Self-pity is a uniquely human characteristic. As D.H. Lawrence expressed in this remarkable little poem:

> *I never saw a wild thing*
> *sorry for itself.*
> *A small bird will drop frozen dead from a bough*
> *without ever having felt sorry for itself.*

Self-pity is an entirely rational response to a pitiless world, but it's not the only response. You can wallow in self-pity as long as you feel the need to. But when you're ready, you can choose a different path. You can ask yourself the question that opens this chapter, a question worth repeating as often as you need it:

## What am I going to do about it?

Time and chance happen to us all. Our personal world is constantly being upended and remade, whether from a global crisis or the details and drama of daily living. During that process, life has a way of relentlessly eliminating our options. That's the bad news, but the good news is we can create new options. New choices. New beginnings.

The answer to helplessness and self-pity is always a question. In one form or another, it's always the same question: the one above.

Whatever happens to you in life, you're free to choose how you respond. That is the single greatest power you possess.

*Magic Questions* unlock that power.

# 3

# How do I change?

When you watch the waves pounding the shore at the beach, they seem irresistible, unpredictable, unstoppable. If you've ever been knocked down by one, it feels like the end of the world. You're slammed and dragged and scraped across the bottom by forces beyond your control. You feel helpless. You can't breathe.

In contrast, if you know what you're doing, you can ride a wave without being consumed by it. You can surf what to others seems like chaos.

As the coronavirus rolled across the planet like the tallest wave in history it presented us with a choice of historic proportions: Will we ride the wave or be consumed by it? It forced us to consider not only how to makes changes in our lives, but how to survive the massive changes imposed upon us.

Choice is the ultimate survival tool. Other animals are programmed by their instinct to survive. Our survival instinct is to program ourselves. We do it by making choices. What we do, where we live, who we live with, what we wear, what we feel, what we eat, what we think, and a thousand other details of living. Uniquely it seems, we have been given the luxury of choice.

But nature played a trick on us. By giving us the freedom to choose, nature forced us to choose. Choice is not a luxury at all: It's a requirement of being human. Like it or not, we have no choice but to make choices. Even if we refuse to choose, that too is a choice.

In the seventeenth century, Descartes famously declared, "I think therefore I am."[1] As profound as that might be, I prefer to look at life this way:

*I think therefore I choose.*

If you want to change something in your life—or survive change that is forced upon you—you need new choices. If you want new choices, you need to ask yourself new questions. Choice is the key to change, but questions are the key to choice.

See for yourself. Ask this question:

## What would I like to change about my life?

If that seems overwhelming, don't worry. Just listen to your answers and capture them—all of them. Use the *Magic Worksheet*™ at the end of this book (or the end of this link: https://www.keithellis.com/magic-worksheet). Take as long as you need. Let your imagination run wild.

### *Imagination*

Speaking of imagination, some people think they don't have any. Ironically, that's a figment of their imagination. The human brain is a volcano of imagination, and that includes your brain. If you've ever had a dream, then you know how true that is. The trick is to harness your imagination in your daily life.

You can begin by admitting your brain is designed to make things up. Imagination is in your DNA. You can't take credit for that, but you can take advantage of it. Ask yourself useful questions.

When you do, your instinct will take over and fill in the blanks. Call it imagination, call it creativity, or call it magic.

Whatever you call it, your brain is hardwired to answer your questions. All you have to do is ask and listen. The more you practice, the better you'll get. Think of your imagination as a muscle, your mental core. When you exercise it, it gets stronger.

*Magic Questions* help exercise your imagination. Consider the list you just created of changes you'd like to make in your life. Choose one.

With that in mind, ask yourself:

## How can I make this change?

Listen to your answers, capture them, and take a moment to reflect on them.

Then ask:

## What would I do first?

Finally, ask this:

## What would help me change?

Listen to your answers, capture them, and reflect. They might surprise you.

### *The Map is Not the Territory*

As amazing as the human brain is, in some ways it's too smart for its own good. When we're born, our brain gets to work building a mental map of our world to cope with the newness and complexity of life as efficiently as possible. We create our own virtual world to help us navigate the real world.

But our mental map also begins to create us. Before we know it, our mental map is such an integral part of who we are that we forget the map is not the territory; it's only a map. [2]

Sometimes we can't tell the difference. When I was in sixth grade, I struck out on a batting tee. Even for a boy whose body was growing faster than his coordination that was hard to do. To make it even more fun, I performed the feat in front of my entire class. They thought it was hilarious. When I swung through that third strike my brain instantly added the experience to my mental map of the world. From then on, I was convinced I couldn't hit a baseball to save my soul.

For years I never bothered to try because my mental map assured me I would fail. It wasn't until high school gym class that I was once again forced to step into the batter's box. I dreaded what I knew was about to happen. If I could strike out on a batting tee, what could I hope to accomplish against a live pitcher? To my amazement, I knocked the next pitch over the fence.

What happened to me during those intervening years? The short answer is that I had grown, but my mental map had not. My hand-eye coordination had finally caught up with my hands and eyes, but my map of the world still had me believing I was that hapless sixth-grader. When our mental map is out of date, it feels like we're trying to navigate Kansas with a map of Mars.

## A Rose by Any Other Frame

The right question would have helped me figure things out a lot sooner. Questions are a great way to update our mental map. They provide a powerful tool for what psychologists call *reframing*.

The meaning we experience in our lives flows from its emotional and psychological context. When we change the context, we change the meaning.[3] Remember Rudolph the Red-Nosed Reindeer? At the beginning of the story, his nose made him an outcast. At the end of the story, his nose made him a hero. The nose didn't change, but the context did. That's the "frame" in which the nose was evaluated. When the context changed, the meaning changed, for Rudolph and everyone else in the story. That's the power of a reframe.

Consider a recent misfortune you've experienced. With that in mind, ask yourself:

## How might that be a good thing?

Give yourself a minute or two to turn it over in your mind. Think of Rudolph's nose.

When you're done with that question, here's a useful variation:

## What might be good about that?

Both are reframing questions. They give you a way to frame a negative into a positive.

### *The Impossibility Filter*

When our mental map gets out of date, we can fall prey to what I call the *impossibility filter.* That's when our subconscious mind won't allow us to imagine choices that our map says are impossible—like me hitting a baseball. This mental processing occurs in the subconscious, so we aren't aware that there's any filtering going on. But we are aware of the results. When we let our mental map get out of date, we condemn ourselves to live in shadows instead of sunshine.

A "What if?" question can help. Think of something you'd like to do, but for whatever reason don't believe you can. Maybe it feels like too great a stretch, or it scares you, or you don't think you have the resources. Maybe someone is telling you'll never be able to pull it off.

With that in mind, ask yourself:

## What if I could do it?

Let that bounce around inside your skull and see what you come up with. Write down whatever thoughts occur to you. Take a moment to reflect on them.

Then ask:

## What would it feel like to do that?

If you like that feeling, ask yourself:

## If I could do that, how would I go about it?

When you were a kid, I bet somebody told you, "You'd be amazed what you can accomplish when you stop telling yourself you can't." Here's your chance.

If you're still stuck, this question can help:

## If anything were possible, what would I do about it?

Ask yourself this question. Give yourself a minute or two to listen, capture, and reflect.

That remarkable phrase —*if anything were possible*— allows us to consider choices that our impossibility filter is hiding from us. You can add this phrase to almost any question and come up with a whole new set of answers.

When you're finished with the questions above, ask this:

## What else could I do?

That's what I call a *cleanup question*. Cleanup questions help you complete the process you begin when you ask yourself a question.

The human brain doesn't reveal everything it knows at the drop of a hat. If someone were to ask you what foods you like, you wouldn't reply with an exhaustive list of everything you've eaten that you happen to enjoy. You'd mention a few of your favorites and leave it at that. If they were then to ask what other foods you like, you'd come up with a few more answers. The two of you could repeat this process for as long as you want, but you would probably run out of patience before you ran out of answers.

When I ask myself cleanup questions, I'm amazed what didn't occur to me the first time around. It's like looking for something you've lost, failing to find it, and then it finally turns up where you hadn't yet looked. Cleanup questions let you keep looking.

### The Critical Difference

When you ask yourself a question, you ask your imagination to come up with some answers. At that point you have a choice. Either you can listen to what your imagination gives you or you can criticize your ideas as they come to you. The moment you begin to criticize, you signal to your imagination that you're done listening. Like an obedient servant, it will shut up and leave you alone. If you want your imagination to do its job, listen to what it has to say. You can pass judgment later.

### Capture Your Future

Capturing ideas is as important as coming up with them in the first place. When you ask yourself a *Magic Question*, the goal is to capture everything your imagination gives you, even the answers that seem silly or impossible.

Don't pretend you'll remember your answers later. You won't. Earl Nightingale, a great philosopher of success, liked to compare an idea to a fish on a hook. Let the fish slip off the hook and it will disappear into the depths, gone forever. He was right. I take that so seriously that I keep a notepad on my nightstand, along with a pen with a built-in LED. When I wake up with an idea in the middle of the night, I can reel it in on the spot.

During the day, I capture my ideas in real time on the notes app on my phone or watch. I use the built-in voice recognition because I can talk faster than I can type. If you prefer to type, or use good old fashioned pen and paper, go for it. Do whatever works for you. If you don't know what works for you, then ask:

### How can I capture ideas whenever they come to me?

How you answer this might be the most important thing you do today.

When you ask yourself a question, answers begin to appear immediately. They may keep appearing for hours, maybe days, while your subconscious continues to work the problem. Be ready to capture your ideas at a moment's notice, at any time of the night or day, especially when you're not thinking about the question. For some reason, the brain loves to answer questions about one thing when you're thinking about something else or nothing at all. That's why people so often experience insights while on a walk, or taking a shower, or staring at the ocean. Be prepared for those magical moments. That's your imagination trying to give you a gift.

When you you've captured all the ideas you want, that's when you can shift into a different gear and begin to evaluate them. At that point, some of your ideas might seem silly. So what? They didn't cost you anything. Some of your ideas might seem impossible. Don't fall for that—that's fear and ignorance talking. "Impossible" ideas are often our best, but we're so quick to dismiss them that we never give them a chance. Put them aside for now. We'll come back to them later.

Happily, not all your ideas will seem silly or impossible. In the process of sorting through them, you may discover exactly what you're looking for. That's why you capture everything your imagination has to say.

### *Let the Air Out of the Tires*

The right question can help you discover entirely unexpected ideas. Consider the answers you came up with for any of the questions you asked yourself above. Glance over them. Now ask this:

## What haven't I thought of?

Treat this like an entirely new question. Listen, capture, and reflect.

When you're done, you'll have some new items for your list: Items that for one reason or another didn't occur to you the first time around. If you keep asking yourself this question, you'll keep getting new answers. Your brain will continue to come up with ideas that, for one reason or another, didn't occur to you the second time around, or the third, and so on. Think of it as a general-purpose cleanup question that can help you discover additional answers for any question you've already asked. Human beings can never have all the answers, but we can always come up with more.

If this seems too easy, it is. Questions are easy to ask, and new options are easy to imagine, but only if you allow yourself the freedom to consider any possibility. Whenever you think you're finished, it never hurts to ask another cleanup question.

Better yet, why not ask your brain to boldly go where no brain has gone before? Consider a change you'd like to make in your life and look at it from an entirely new angle:

## What are some unconventional possibilities?

Listen, capture, and reflect. Give yourself a minute or two to come up with some answers.

This potent question dares you to think differently than you normally do. It challenges you to consider possibilities you would not normally consider—maybe no one would consider. It gives you permission to imagine the problem from an entirely different point of view.

Albert Einstein is a good example. As a sixteen-year-old boy, he imagined what it would be like to ride alongside a beam of light traveling at the same speed. That shift in perspective contradicted the conventional Newtonian view of the universe. Within a few years, Einstein's thought experiment had evolved into an unconventional solution to those problems, his theory of special relativity.[4] That solution changed the world.

Sometimes all it takes to solve a problem is to examine it from an unorthodox perspective. To get in the mood for that, I like to recall an old story about a tractor-trailer that was wedged under a bridge. Police and firefighters were out in force, trying to figure out how to remove the truck without damaging it or the bridge, but none of them knew what to do. One of the bystanders was a little girl. She tugged at her mother's hand and asked, "Why don't they just let the air out of the tires?"

# 4

# How do I decide?

*a*s wonderful as it is to have new choices to consider, we still have to decide which ones to pursue. Computers suggest a nifty way to do that, even if you don't know anything about them.

Conventional computers are programmed with a series of binary digits called *bits*. A bit is either a 1 or a 0. It acts like a digital version of an on/off switch. Computers break down even the most complex operations into a series of these switches to enable the most sophisticated technology we have, from space travel to genetic engineering.

Binary choices are also a useful way for human beings to make decisions. Our mental processes are more sophisticated than even the most powerful computer, yet we can improve our decision-making by focusing on only two alternatives at a time.

Consider one of the lists of answers you captured in the previous chapter. With that list in hand, follow these steps:

1.  Number the items on your list.
2.  Compare *Item 1* with *Item 2* by asking: **Which of these two options do I prefer?**

3. Take the item you choose and compare it to the next item on your list. Ask the same question.
4. Repeat this process until you've gone through your list.

When you're finished, you'll find that something amazing has happened. You've identified the top-ranked item on your list. Based on head-to-head competition with the other items on your list, you've declared one the winner. Think of it as your *first choice*. Write *#1* beside it.

Rank the rest of the list. Set aside your first choice and repeat the process for the items that remain. When you determine your *second choice*, rank it *#2* and set it aside. Repeat the process until you've ranked all the items on your list.

As simple as this process is, it works with any size list for any kind of decision. If it feels familiar, it's how champions get crowned in many tournaments. Competitors pair off in head-to-head competition and the winner moves on to the next round. The process is repeated until there's only one competitor left standing. If it works for Major League Baseball, March Madness, and the North American Debating Championship, it will work for you. The more decisions you can reduce to A-to-B comparisons, the easier it will be to make choices.

But there's a catch. Even when you narrow down a decision to a comparison between two items, you still have to decide. It may be easy, but what if it's not? Here's a question that gets to the heart of the matter:

## Which option do I feel better about?

You've probably been told a thousand times to listen to your gut. This is how you do that.

Here's a variation on the theme:

### How does this option make me feel?

If option A leaves you feeling warm and fuzzy all over while option B has you feeling guilty and conflicted, then your unconscious mind is trying to tell you something. Might be a good idea to listen.

Here's a different approach:

### If a friend had to make this decision, what would I recommend?

Most of us would rather give advice than follow it. Why not give yourself advice? Pretend you're giving it to someone else. That new point of view might be exactly what you need.

### *The Truth of Consequences*

Decisions have consequences. One way to weigh your options is to weigh their consequences:

### If I choose this option, what are the consequences?

When you've answered that question, do the same for the second option. When you're done, compare the consequences of each option and you'll have a clearer idea of how to make a decision.

Our ability to evaluate consequences doesn't come easily; at least not at first. When we're children, we tend to make choices without much thought about consequences. We go to school on a cold day without thinking to take a jacket. We watch TV or play video games instead of doing homework. We're happy to eat hot fudge sundaes and chocolate chip cookies every day.

To grow up is to become aware of consequences. If we eat too much, we gain weight. If we don't dress for the weather, we feel miserable. If we choose to play video games or watch TV instead of doing our work, then we fail in school or the workplace. The level of emotional maturity we reach as adults, whatever that might be, is directly related to our ability to take consequences into account when we make decisions.

Here's a question that takes this maturity to a whole new level:

## If I choose this option, what are the unintended consequences?

Every choice we make is a cause that sets in motion effects both large and small. We anticipate some of the effects, but many are unintended. Cause and effect are so complex that we can't know in advance every effect of the causes we set in motion. Yet we'll make better decisions if we attempt to understand their unintended consequences. As the old saying goes: be careful what you wish for because you just might get it.

### *The Goldilocks Protocol*

When we're torn between two choices, sometimes it helps to split the difference. Choice A may feel like too much but choice B may feel like too little. The best choice may be somewhere in the middle— like Goldilocks, we want something that's just right. That's why coffee shops offer drinks in at least three sizes. Too large a dose of caffeine might send you bouncing off the walls. Too small, and it won't get your motor running. But medium, ah, that's perfect.

The Goldilocks Protocol can help with even the most challenging decisions. Consider a relationship you're struggling with. Option A is to live with it and accept the status quo. Option B is to end it once and for all. But before you resign yourself to one choice or the other, ask this:

## What is the middle ground?

Listen to your answers. Capture them and reflect on them.

Your answers will likely depend on the circumstances. If it's a personal relationship, maybe the middle ground is to see a counselor. If it's a professional relationship, you could find someone to serve as your mentor, or someone to act as a referee. In either situation, the middle ground might be to see a little less of the other person—or maybe a little more.

Here's another example. Suppose you're trying to figure out where to live. Should you move to the country, far from your office, to a place where homes cost less but require a longer commute? Or should you move to the city and live nearer to where you work? You'll pay more, but you'll have a shorter commute. In a case like that, there is literally and figuratively a middle ground between those options: a location somewhere between the country and the city. That's where suburbs come from.

Or you could try an entirely new wrinkle and think about working from home. Then your commute no longer matters. That option might never have occurred to you unless you stopped to explore the middle ground.

The Goldilocks Protocol is very useful, so let's look at one more example. Suppose you're thinking about retirement. If you narrow your choices to only two extremes—work or no work—you may force yourself in a direction you're not ready to go. But if you explore the middle ground, you might discover interesting alternatives you hadn't considered.

For instance, you might work part time. Or maybe you could leave your current job and sell yourself back to your employer as a consultant. You'd be doing the same work, but you'd be working for yourself, calling the shots, and you might make more money. That feeling alone, of calling your own shots, can extend a career for years without extending the mental grind of working for someone else. Or you might explore an entirely different career. If you've been in the business world, you could turn to public service. If you've been in public service, you could turn to business. Or maybe you could work from home. That's not retirement, but compared to commuting every day it might feel like it.

Despite all the tools we've discussed in this chapter, what if you still can't decide? Try this question:

## If I could decide, what would I choose?

*"What if"* questions have a way of unlocking what's on our mind.

If you still can't decide between two options, then it doesn't matter which one you choose, does it? If one choice seems every bit as appealing as the other, then pick one and move on. Or choose to do nothing. It's easy to forget that's also a choice. If you come to a crossroads and can't decide which way to go, then you've chosen to stand there.

When you're tired of standing there, flip a coin. Think of it as a way to overcome the inertia of indecision. If a coin flip feels random, it's anything but. The trick is to pay attention to which choice you're subconsciously rooting for while the coin is in the air. That's the one you want, even if it's hard to admit it.

Another way to make up your mind is to ask a better question to help you choose between two options. Like this:

## Which one can I live without?

Trust your gut. If you still can't decide, choose one anyway and move on. If your gut says you've made the wrong choice, you can always switch to the other one and then move on for real.

---

5

---

## How can I change my life at the speed of thought?

*Y*ou are what you think about. If you want to change your life at the speed of thought, change your thoughts. If you want to change your thoughts, change your questions. Life really is as simple as that.

That doesn't mean it's easy. You can't change everything at once just by changing your thoughts any more than you can fly from New York to Tokyo just by thinking about it. But your thoughts are what set you in motion.

A Taoist proverb says a journey of a thousand miles begins with a single step. When you change your thoughts you take that first step.

Here's a good place to start:

### What am I thinking right now?

As busy as we are, we're not always aware what we're thinking about. Thought often flows from habit, and habit is largely unconscious.

To change your thinking, it helps to know what you're thinking about. If your thoughts are unhappy, depressed, or angry, you'll feel that way as well. If you think self-defeating thoughts, you'll engage in self-defeating behavior. If you think you're helpless, you'll feel and act that way. Your feelings and action don't just happen—they flow from what you think about.

When your thoughts aren't helping you, think about something else. Ask yourself:

## What else can I think about?

Treat this as a brainstorming question. Listen to your answers. Imagine the enormous range of thoughts you could be thinking. Capture some and reflect on them. You may be surprised how different you feel.

Here's a useful variation:

## What would I rather think about?

Let your mind wander; that's the point. Give yourself at least a minute to have fun with this. Capture your ideas as you go.

Here's a different approach:

## What thoughts will take me where I want to be?

If you discover thoughts that are more satisfying than what you started with, ask:

## How can I think this way more often?

Sometimes it feels like your mind has a mind of its own. You may find yourself clinging to unpleasant thoughts, wallowing in them until that particular emotional flame burns itself out. You can wait around for that if you like, or you can take conscious control of the process.

For instance, if your mind resists the question, "What else can I think about?" ask the same question in "What if?" form:

If I could think of something else, what would it be?

When you think differently you change what you feel, what you do, and who you are. From the first word to the last, that's what this book is all about.

When in doubt, the easiest way to change your thinking is to ask yourself a *Magic Question*. Like this one:

What *Magic Questions* will help me with this?

## 6

# What is my purpose?

*S*ome people are lucky. They know their purpose. They know who they are and what they're meant to do. For the rest of us, sooner or later we're bound to wonder: *"Isn't there more to life?"*

Of course there is. But here's a more useful question:

## What more do I want from life?

Give yourself a minute or two to answer this, and another minute to reflect on what you come up with.

Most of us have no trouble supplying surface answers to this question. We want a new job, better relationships, more money, and a cherry on top. But sooner or later, we realize those things aren't enough. We have to dig deeper:

## What is my purpose in life?

Listen, really listen to what you have to say. Capture everything you come up with.

When it comes to purpose we seem to have a hidden filter, as if our subconscious won't allow us to consider thoughts that might shake up our lives. Imagine if one moment you were an investment banker, and the next you wanted to teach yoga. That would be distracting.

But that's the point. We owe it to ourselves and our fellow human beings to become distracted by our purpose. Nothing else comes close. Nothing else can give us the life most worth living.

When we wonder if there's more to life what we're looking for is a sense of purpose. As enjoyable as it is to have fine relationships, success in our career, and material prosperity, human beings want more. We yearn to be part of something greater than ourselves, whether it's a family, a community, an organization, a social revolution, an inflection point in history, or some useful contribution to the greater good. We want life to mean something. Meaning flows from purpose. Until we discover our purpose, we will never stop wondering if there's more to life.

If you don't know your purpose, then your purpose is to discover it.

Here's another *Magic Question* that can help:

## What would I like to accomplish with my life?

Take a moment to jot down some answers. Don't judge them; just listen.

When you're done, and only when you're done, ask yourself this:

## When I look back on my life, what will I wish I had accomplished?

You know the drill. Ask, listen, capture, and reflect—especially the listen part.

When you finish answering this, compare your two lists. These may seem to be the same question, but they often elicit different answers.

The change in perspective taps into something different inside of us. When we look forward, we tend to have a shorter time horizon. We may have a clear idea of what we want to accomplish in the next few months or years, but beyond that, not so much. When we look backward, we feel as if we're looking at a much longer timeframe. All bets are off. Who knows what you might be able to accomplish with an entire lifetime at your disposal?

The difference between how you answer the first question and the second is a measure of your uncertainty about what you want from life. When there's no difference between looking forward and backward, you know what you want. You know who you are. You know your purpose, even if you've never called it that before.

Here's another approach:

## How would I like to be remembered?

Ask, listen, capture, and reflect. This moment can change your life. Give yourself time to take advantage of it.

Now ask yourself this intriguing variation:

## If I had to write my own obituary, what would I like it to say?

Go ahead, write your fantasy obituary. There's no better way to understand who you'd like to be than to imagine who you wish you'd been.

Once you have something on paper, close your eyes and take a few deep breaths. Open them and read what you've written as if you're seeing it for the first time. Read it out loud for good measure.

Is it the person you'd like to be?

If so, then ask this incredibly powerful *Magic Question* you already know so well:

## What am I going to do about it?

Here's another approach:

If this were the last day of my life, how would I spend it?

Take as long as you need to capture your answers. It's a great way to cut through the clutter of life and discover what really matters to you.

With that list in mind, ask:

How can I fit more of those activities into every day?

When you know what matters to you, you can organize your life around it.

Here's one of the most useful questions to discover your purpose:

How can I help make the world a better place?

Ask, listen, capture, and reflect.

When you're finished, let your answers settle in for a moment. They may surprise you.

To make the world better, you don't have to sell all your possessions and give the money to charity; just be the best version of who you are. Pursue what you're passionate about. If you live a life full of the purpose you've chosen, you'll make the world a better place. You'll become the person you imagine yourself to be. The world needs more people like that.

While you're getting to know yourself, here's a question that will rock your world:

What's important to me?

Spend a few minutes with this. Rank your answers in order of their importance to you. You'll be amazed what you learn.

When you're done, and you have a good idea what's important to you, ask yourself:

## What do I care about?

Listen to your answers and capture them.

When you're finished, compare these answers with your answers to the previous question. The first question asks for a value judgment. The second asks how you feel. On one hand you're asking your brain; on the other you're asking your heart. Why not get input from both?

Here's a question that approaches it from an entirely different angle:

## What interests me?

If you want to learn something interesting about yourself, make a list of what interests you. Rank it. Let it stare back at you for a moment and sink in.

Self, meet self.

If you were asked to describe yourself, you'd probably respond with something like a Facebook post designed for public consumption. We all want to position ourselves favorably to the rest of the world. Even the obituary you wrote for yourself was probably for public consumption. But in the privacy of your own mind, when you ask yourself what you're interested in, you get a clear picture of who you are. Not who you want to be, not how you want to be perceived, but who you are.

Here's a question that offers a unique approach to the process of self discovery:

## What do I want to be when I grow up?

Most of us stopped paying attention to this question when adults stopped asking us. But it never gets old; after all, we never finish growing up. It may even be more useful to us now than it was when we were kids because it reminds us we still have room to grow. To paraphrase Robert Frost, we have promises to keep, and choices to make before we sleep.

Go ahead, have fun with this question. Listen to your answers. Give yourself a chance to reflect. The better you know yourself, the more likely you are to get what you want from life instead of what you don't.

# 7

## What if I do know the answer?

*S*ooner or later when you ask yourself a *Magic Question* your brain will respond with something like this: *What if I don't know the answer?* That's your subconscious telling you to knock on some other door. It's not looking for answers; it's trying to avoid them by filling you with doubt. As Shakespeare said, "Our doubts are traitors and make us lose the good we oft might win by fearing to attempt."[1]

For any useful question you ask yourself, your subconscious can deflect it with a question of its own. I call it an *interference pattern*. To deal with it, keep asking yourself questions designed to find answers rather than avoid them. Sooner or later your subconscious will get the hint.

For example, here's the negative "What if?" question from above:

*What if I don't know the answer?*

Here's a useful response:

What if I do know the answer?

Even better:

If I knew the answer, what would it be?

Or my favorite:

If I weren't afraid to know the answer, what would it be?

Here's another negative question:

*What if it's impossible?*

Here's the obvious response:

What if it's possible?

Or this:

If anything were possible, what would I do?

Here's one more negative question:

*What if I can't do it?*

Here's a useful response:

What if I could do it?

Or this:

If I could do it, how would I go about it?

Useful questions enable change. Negative ones prevent it. Useful questions expand our possibilities. Negative ones limit them. Useful questions focus on what we can do. Negative ones focus on what we can't.

A useful question takes us where we want to go. A negative question freezes us in place, like a lion's roar freezes a gazelle long enough for the lion to kill it. From one moment to the next each of us has the power to choose which kind of questions we ask ourselves. Choose wisely.

## 8

## What can I live without?

*T*he first time I pruned a rosebush, the process seemed counterintuitive. There I was, butchering a living thing in order to help it thrive. How could that possibly work? Yet thrive it did.

In every life there comes a time for pruning. When we leave behind what we can live without, we make more room for what's important to us, for what we care about, for what interests us. We give ourselves the chance to thrive.

Choose one of the lists you've made about what you want from life. Ask this question about the first item on your list:

*Can I live without this?*

If the answer is yes, cross off that item and move to the next. Repeat the process for the entire list. When you've jettisoned everything you don't need, you'll finally have time for what you do.

When you ask yourself what you can live without, it helps to ask the mirror-image question:

## What can't I live without?

Spend time with this. Listen, capture, and reflect. Decide what isn't negotiable in your life. Everything else is.

Now comes the hard part. Sometimes these decisions are made for us; the pruning happens whether we like it or not.

When COVID-19 hit, the entire world had to face what it was forced to live without. Billions of people asked themselves questions they never wanted to ask:

- *How can I provide for my family without income?*
- *How can I live without seeing and touching the people I love?*
- *How can I survive?*

Yet even painful questions have answers. They can show us the light at the end of the tunnel.

When you face circumstances beyond your control, let the magic in you shine. Let your brain do what it does best. Ask the hard questions and listen to your answers. From out of the ashes, create new choices for yourself.

You may be surprised by what you can live without, and value all the more what you can't.

# 9

## How can I turn this into a Magic Question?

*M*agic *Questions* are like armor-piercing shells that help you penetrate mental obstacles such as complacency, ignorance, fear, and self-doubt. They're usually open-ended questions; you're not looking for a yes or no answer.

For example, instead of a closed-ended question like this—*Is this going to get me the job I want?*—a *Magic Question* is open-ended, like this:

### How can I get the job I want?

The first question is binary; it elicits a yes or no answer. The second elicits information and ideas. That's the difference between a *Magic Question* and a binary question.

Yes-or-no questions can paint you into a corner. If the answer is no, it does away with any attempt to find your way to yes, and vice versa.

To be sure, some questions need to be answered with yes or no, or with a binary choice between option A or B. These can be valuable questions, but they aren't *Magic Questions.*

Here's another example. Suppose someone offers you a job. You

46

can ask yourself a binary question like this—do I accept this offer or not? It's an important decision to make, but it's not a *Magic Question*.

On the other hand, *Magic Questions* can help you consider the offer:

What kind of a job do I want?

What do I want to do with my life?

Where do I want to do it?

How can I get a better offer?

Open-ended questions are discovery questions. We use them to learn more about ourselves and discover options. Closed-ended questions are decision questions. We use them to decide between options. Ultimately, we need both types of questions, but change begins with *Magic Questions*.

When you have a problem to solve, a challenge to confront, or an opportunity to make the most of, ask yourself:

How can I turn this into a *Magic Question*?

For instance, if you need to solve a problem, you could ask:

How can I solve that?

That's the most obvious question, but it works.

There are as many variations as you have time to dream them up, such as:

What is a better way to solve this?

How would I feel if I solved this?

How would my mother, father, grandparent, coach, mentor, or best friend solve this?

Who can help me solve this?

If I could solve this, how would I go about it?

In like manner, you can frame any challenge as a question:

How can I meet this challenge?

Or:

How can I overcome this?

You can also use any of the variations above and rephrase them for challenges rather than problems.

If you have an opportunity, you can ask:

How can I make the most of this?

Or try the variations above, rephrased for opportunities.

You can even turn the process of asking questions into a question:

What is a useful variation on that question?

What is another question I can ask myself?

What is a good follow up question?

Whatever life throws at you, when you know how to ask *Magic Questions*, you can fill your life with magic answers.

# 10

# What is the most important thing for me to do right now?

*H*ave you ever finished a busy day and wondered if you actually accomplished anything? Given how crowded our lives have become, that's easy to do.

But busyness isn't the problem. The real challenge is how to separate what's urgent from what's important. Most of us do it on the fly, as a matter of habit. The unfortunate result is that we tend to prioritize the urgent at the expense of what really matters to us.

Case in point: Your boss assigns you a high-priority project that's due in two weeks. If you're successful with it you'll get a promotion. Later that day, your boss asks you to do something that has to be completed by tomorrow. Which do you work on first?

Most of us would drop what we're doing and focus on the task that has to be completed by tomorrow. That's why most of us live empty, meaningless lives full of mindless activity.

Just kidding. But if that tease cuts close to the bone, this might be the most important chapter in the book. The urgent always wins unless we make time for what's important.

When in doubt, ask yourself:

## What is the most important thing for me to do?

Listen to your answers. Capture them. Rank them in order of their importance to you. If you want a refresher on how to do that, review Chapter 4 of Book I, *"How do I decide?"*

When we think about what's important to us, it's easy to get flooded with ideas. If they're all important, it's tempting to treat them the same. But they aren't. Spend the time necessary to prioritize your list. Once you've identified item #1, start working on it. Think of it as your *First Thing*; it's the most important thing for you to do. If you'd like your life to turn out the way you want, do first things first.

Sometimes that's easier said than done. Wherever this chapter finds you in life, you probably have things you're already committed to. If your calendar is full, ask:

## How can I do my First Thing first?

This is where the rubber meets the road. Your job is to make time for what's most important to you. If you don't, who will?

I schedule my First Thing for first thing in the morning. That's when I'm freshest and least likely to have a scheduling conflict.

That was a big change for me. I used to read the paper while I ate breakfast. I loved it, but it consumed a large chunk of the most productive time of my day. So I changed my schedule. Now when I get up in the morning I get right to work. That small change had a profound impact. I can't wait to start work in the morning because I get to do my First Thing first. I begin my day doing what's most important to me. That's the best motivational trick I know.

Whatever time works best for you, put your First Thing on your calendar. Whether you use a calendar app, a day timer, a desktop calendar, or a clay tablet, block out time each day to work on your First Thing. If it's not something you can finish in one sitting, break it into smaller chunks and schedule those.

Schedule at least twenty minutes a day for your First Thing.

Regardless of what else is going on in your life, at least you'll make progress every day on what's most important to you. In the process, you'll turn first things first into a habit—the most useful habit there is.

When you schedule time for your First Thing, honor your commitment. For some reason, the appointments we make with ourselves tend to be less of a priority than the appointments we make with others. If this happens to you, think of a first-thing appointment as a meeting with the most important person in the world. Consider it a matter of self respect. If you don't show up for a meeting with yourself, why would anyone else?

When I schedule a First Thing for any time other than first thing in the morning, I set an alarm on my phone. That keeps me on track during even the busiest of days. I made it a habit. You can, too.

Your priorities may shift with time and context. Events, both good and bad, have a way of redefining what's important. To take context into account, ask yourself this question:

## What is the most important thing for me to do right now?

Your answers may differ from what you came up with in response to the initial question above. That's because you've added a timeframe.

Time is not fungible. The thirty seconds before they close the door of the airplane you're trying to board are not equal to the thirty seconds of the commercial interrupting your favorite TV show.

If you're driving in a snowstorm, the most important thing you can do is drive safely. When you get where you're going, something else will become more important, such as getting inside.

From time to time during the day, it's useful to check and see if you're working on your First Thing. This question can help:

What could I be doing now that's more important?

Or this interesting variation:

What's a better way to spend my time?

If you don't know your First Thing, your First Thing is to figure it out. Only you know what's important to you. Only you can decide if you'll ever get around to it.

# 11

# What am I afraid of?

*M*illions of years ago, our ancestors evolved a life-saving response to the threats they faced in a dangerous world. Respiration accelerated to increase the supply of oxygen. Heart rate and blood pressure increased to direct more blood to the muscles. The brain flooded the bloodstream with chemicals that equipped the body for fight or flight.

That response is still with us today, but the threats have changed. Fear amps up our bodies for fight or flight the way it did when we had to confront saber-toothed tigers, but it doesn't do us much good in a job interview, speaking in front of a group, facing a difficult decision, or on a date. Our ancient physiological response to what we fear can cause us to overreact—or worse, to avoid situations that frighten us. That's the real problem. Fear can keep you from living the life you dream of; it can even keep you from dreaming it.

There are many levels of fear, from mild anxiety to heart-pounding phobia. Most of our fear, like an iceberg, is below the surface. It grows in dark places, in the cracks and crevices of our subconscious, sabotaging our lives while we remain largely unaware of its presence. That's what gives fear so much power; it's shadowy existence makes it difficult to confront.

The first step in dealing with fear is to get it out in the open. If you feel something holding you back, or making you hesitate, that's a good time to ask:

## What am I afraid of?

Listen to what you have to say. Capture it. In the light of day, when a fear stares back at you from a piece of paper or a computer screen, it might not feel so intimidating.

Ask yourself:

## What if I weren't afraid?

Try that on for size. Then follow-up with this:

## How would I feel if I weren't afraid?

Let yourself dwell on that feeling. If you like it, keep it.

Not all fear disappears when you expose it to sunlight. Some things in life you just have to do scared. That's when it helps to ask this question:

## How can I use my fear to do what I'm afraid of?

There's a fine line between fear and excitement. When you feel fear, your body is preparing to fight or run away. Think of all that energy just begging to be used.

Ask yourself:

## How can I take advantage of that energy?

You don't have to be an adrenaline junkie to use adrenaline to your advantage. You just have to channel it so it propels you forward instead of backward.

Like this:

### How can I use fear to fuel courage?

Courage isn't the absence of fear—it's the willingness to do what you're afraid of. When you commit to that, adrenaline becomes your friend rather than your enemy.

That's why adrenaline junkies do what they do; not because they're tempting fate, but because they've learned that when you act despite your fear, you transform fear into an unbelievable source of energy.

### *Hard Answers*

When we begin asking ourselves *Magic Questions*, we may be afraid to ask the hard questions because we're afraid of hard answers. If that happens to you, ask this:

### If I weren't afraid to know the answer, what would I come up with?

You may learn something important about yourself. You may discover options you didn't know you had. Act on them or not, it's up to you. Either way, you're making the decision, instead of allowing hidden fears to make it for you.

# 12

# How can I turn Magic Questions into a habit?

*C*ongratulations! You've finished *Book I*. You've earned a PhD in how to create the life you want. Time to take a break from learning and focus on doing.

Start with this:

### How can I turn *Magic Questions* into a habit?

When I was a teenager I wanted to play guitar. I tried to teach myself several times, but each time, after a few days of frustration and sore fingertips, I gave up. When I went to college I shared this story with a musician friend of mine. His response surprised me. "I can teach you how to play guitar in a month," he said, "but if you want me to give you lessons, you have to agree to practice every day, for at least twenty minutes a day, for thirty days in a row. If you miss a day, you promise to start over."

That seemed like a dream come true. Twenty minutes a day to learn how to play guitar?

I took him up on it, and as you might imagine it turned out to be harder than I thought. With a schedule full of classes, studying, exams, not to mention parties, those twenty minutes a day proved to be more elusive than I had anticipated. Obviously, my friend knew that would be the case, which is why he made me promise to start over if I missed a day. That commitment kept me on the straight and narrow for the full thirty days.

Sure enough, in a month I could play guitar. I was no rock star, but I knew enough chords and finger patterns to play lots of songs. More importantly, I had developed the habit of playing every day. That was the secret, just as my teacher knew it would be.

You can create a habit in thirty days if you follow the same guidelines. Practice your new habit for at least twenty minutes a day for thirty days in a row. Think of it as the *20/30 Plan*. If you miss a day, reset the counter to Day 1, and continue for thirty days in a row.

You can put the same process in motion with *Magic Questions*. For the next thirty days, ask yourself a different question every day. Listen to your answers, capture them, and reflect on what you come up with. If you miss a day, reset the counter to Day 1, and continue for thirty days in a row.

You have plenty to work with. In the previous chapters you've encountered dozens of *Magic Questions*. Hundreds more follow. You can also visit my website *Weekly Magic*™ for a free random question every week:

*www.keithellis.com/weekly-magic*

To get started on your new habit, choose a question to ask yourself today. Maybe it's one you've already found useful, or a new one from the table of contents, or a random question from *Weekly Magic*, or from the *Index of Magic Questions* at the end of this book where we list all the *Magic Questions* you'll find in these pages.

When you've decided which question to ask yourself today, use the *Magic Worksheet* to bring out the full power of the question.

Then schedule a time tomorrow to ask a different question. Write the question on your calendar. Keep this up for thirty days. If you miss a day start over. Reset the counter to Day 1 and continue for thirty days in a row. Before you know it, you'll turn *Magic Questions* into the *Magic Habit.*

# Book II: MAKING MAGIC

# Part 1: The Magic in Me

# 1

# If I could change one thing in my life, what would it be?

*A*sk yourself this question and listen to your answers.

Don't be shocked if you come up with more than one answer, maybe a lot more. That's the fun of asking *"one thing"* questions: there's almost never just one thing.

Capture everything you come up with and rank the items on your list. If you need a refresher on how to do that, revisit Chapter 4, Book I, *"How do I decide?"*

When you're finished, you will have identified the one change you'd most like to make in your life. That's a great place to start. But first, ask yourself this follow-up question:

## If anything were possible, what's one thing in my life I would change?

Listen to your answers, capture them, and rank them.

When you're finished, compare the answers with the previous ones. Any differences you find likely arise from the mental roadblock I've referred to as the impossibility filter. Don't underestimate it.

When you ask young children what they want to be when they grow up, they give you unfiltered answers: A dancer, an astronaut, a movie star. Kids haven't filled their subconscious with all sorts of rules and regulations, so they're less inhibited in their thinking. They don't care about what's impossible; all they care about is what they want. They're at that magical time of life when anything is possible.

So are we. But a funny thing happens to us on the way to adulthood. We get a better sense of what we want to do, and we also get a better sense of what we think we can't do. Too often, we incorporate the latter into our mental map of the world.

For instance, suppose you decided way back in second grade you weren't "creative" because you couldn't draw a cow or dog as well as your classmates did. Through the years, your talent would have outgrown that misconception, if you let it. There are many ways to be creative other than drawing, if you allow yourself to think about them. Unfortunately, your subconscious can get in the way.

Don't let an outdated mental map limit your choices with misconceptions it formed when you were a kid, and thus a very different person physically, intellectually, and emotionally. Use *Magic Questions* to bypass the filters holding you back.

Almost any question beginning with "If" or "What if" can help, not to mention the four powerful words, "If anything were possible…"

Use questions like these to drill down into specific areas of your life where your subconscious filters might be hiding important insights.

If I could change one thing about me, what would it be?

Or turbo charge the question with this:

If anything were possible, what's one thing I would change about me?

We are who we are, until we choose to be different. It's basic math. If you add to your positive qualities or subtract from your negative ones, the result is a better version of you. If you want to become the person you imagine you can be, "One thing" questions empower you to do that, one step at a time.

You can take the same approach at work:

If I could change one thing about my job, what would it be?

Listen, capture, and reflect.

Then ask this followup:

If anything were possible, what's one thing I would change about my job?

I like the one-two punch of asking a "one thing" question and following it up with the "If anything were possible" version. Together, they give me a glimpse of what my internal map of the world thinks I can't do. I've spent too much of my life allowing myself to be limited by that kind of nonsense, so these days I cut to the chase with questions that help me redraw my mental map on the fly.

Speaking of your job, you can't necessarily change everything you want to change if you work for someone else. That's okay. Capture all your answers anyway. What you can't change might give you insight into what you can. Changing anything can give you a sense of empowerment and a new feeling of ownership over what you're doing. If you focus on what you can do instead of what you can't, piece by piece you'll reclaim a sense of control in your work. If push comes to shove and you find yourself in a job that's too limiting, you can always choose to move on.

The "one thing" approach can also help with relationships:

If I could change one thing about this relationship, what would it be?

Capture whatever your brain gives you, prioritize your list, and start with the most important item.

"One thing" questions can help you delve into the nittiest, grittiest details of your life, like this:

If I could change one thing about my daily routine, what would it be?

Or this:

If I could change one thing about my self-image, what would it be?

We expend so much time and energy worrying what the world thinks of us that we sometimes forget what we think of ourselves. Yet that is the core of who we are. There's nothing you can do to guarantee how the world sees you, but how you see yourself is entirely within your control.

Here's a question that can help:

How would I like to see myself?

Your answers will tell you a great deal about yourself. Listen to what you have to say and give yourself time to think about it.

If something jumps out at you, ask:

How can I be more like that?

You can use "one thing" questions to help you get healthy:

If I could change one thing about my lifestyle, what would it be?

Whatever you come up with, you can drill down into it. What you eat, for example:

### If I could change one thing about my eating habits, what would it be?

Whatever you eat, whether it's too much or too little, junk food or healthy food, chances are it's mostly a matter of habit. Whether your goal is to lose weight, gain weight, increase your energy, or improve your health, you can create eating habits that will help you achieve your objective. All you need to do is ask.

As always, you can turbo-charge the question like this:

### If anything were possible, what's one thing I would change about my eating habits?

Here's another important detail of life you can change with a "one thing" question:

### If I could change one thing about my workplace, what would it be?

You can change your workplace without changing your job. You can face in a different direction, swap out your pictures, change your desk, chair, or lighting, or change something else you have control over. Small adjustments in your workplace can produce big results. It can affect your mood, productivity, and sense of expectation about coming to work in the morning. Take advantage of it.

"One thing" questions are a great way to zero in on problems and opportunities in your life.

### If I could solve one problem in my life, what would it be?

Or this:

### If I could focus on one opportunity in my life, what would it be?

When you look at these questions together, they seem like two sides of the same coin. No doubt you've heard the classic reframe, "Don't think of it as a problem, think of it as an opportunity." It's a cliché, but it works. Problems are opportunities. Opportunities are problems waiting to be solved. If you approach the world from both frames, you increase your probability of success.

These are only a few examples of "one thing" questions. This question can help you discover more:

What other areas of my life could use a "one thing" makeover?

## 2

# How can I cause the effect I desire?

*E*verything we do sets in motion a cause that produces an effect. To get what we want from life, we have only to set in motion the causes that will produce the effects we desire.

Think of something you want to accomplish in your personal life, career, or community. With that in mind, ask yourself:

### What cause can I set in motion to produce that effect?

Give yourself a minute or two to come up with ideas. Treat it like a brainstorming exercise.

When you're done, notice that your answers speak to what you *can* do instead of what you *can't*. Our brains have a gift for jumping to conclusions about the road ahead. This mountain is too high to climb. This river is too wide to cross. These obstacles we're facing are too difficult. But when we think in terms of cause and effect, we change the dynamic. "Can't" becomes irrelevant when we begin with the assumption we *can*.

Once you throw this switch in your brain, you'll never be powerless again. You'll become a participant in your life instead of a spectator. You'll stack the deck in your favor by focusing your intellect and energy on how to get what you want instead of reasons why you can't.

If at any point you don't like where your life is headed, ask yourself:

What cause can I set in motion that will produce the outcome I desire?

Or this:

How can I change the outcome by changing the cause?

You can combine these two questions into one that is even more powerful:

How can I cause the effect I desire?

This is one of those questions that can be used in almost any situation. Practice it. When you turn it into a habit, you'll be in the driver's seat for the rest of your life.

---

3

# What have I learned from this?

---

*W*hen he made a mistake, a friend of mine used to say, "I've never had any education I didn't have to pay for." The bigger the mistake, the more he learned from the experience.

Get what you pay for. When you make a mistake, ask yourself:

## What have I learned from this?

Just make sure you learn the right lesson instead of the wrong one. Remember the first time you touched a hot stove when you were a kid? Maybe you don't, but your fingers do, and you've tried to avoid that mistake ever since. But you haven't avoided stoves.

If you want to learn something useful from an experience, add "useful" to your *Magic Question*:

## What is something useful I can learn from this?

Imagine a life in which in which you can learn from your mistakes the same way you learned not to touch a hot stove. Make it a habit by asking questions like these:

What did I learn that can help me next time?

What did I learn about anticipating problems before they arise?

What did I learn that will make me better at this?

Here's a question that puts a different spin on things:

What do I wish I'd learned before this happened?

We have 20/20 vision in hindsight. Why not turn hindsight into foresight? It's a great way to approach your next project or tackle an obstacle.

So is this:

What do I need to learn about this that I don't yet know?

Making a mistake can teach us a lesson. But what if we could learn the lesson before we make the mistake? It's possible, if we ask the right questions.

4

# How would I like to feel right now?

*W*hen we're swept away in a river of negative emotion, we might think our first instinct would be to swim ashore. Instead, we often choose to wallow in it. Emotions have an inertia that defies sober reflection. Like wildfires, they rage until they burn themselves out.

If you'd rather not wait that long, you need to learn how to fight these wildfires. As much time as we spend thinking about the way we feel, we may not realize we feel the way we think. The easiest way to feel differently is to think differently. If you want to experience a new emotion, choose a new thought.

Here's a question that can help:

## What color is the ceiling?

What's it got to do with anything? Nothing, and that's the point. If you want to feel differently, think about something else. As a bonus, when you look up you access another part of your brain. You can't help but feel a change.

You can also ask a more direct question:

## How would I like to feel right now?

You may not get a clear answer at first because your current emotions might not want to let you slip away that easily. You can short-circuit this dynamic by asking:

## When this is over, how would I like to feel?

This question acknowledges your emotions' right to exist. Meanwhile, you give yourself permission to think about a more useful emotion, one that you'd like to feel when this particular wildfire is out.

As it happens, our brains can't think of another emotion in any meaningful way without feeling it, if only a little. That may be all it takes to break free from the grip of a negative emotion.

Or not. Emotions are stubborn things. Most of the time we want to feel what we're feeling, even when we feel bad. Why else would legions of moviegoers seek out tearjerkers and horror movies? The same dynamic is true for all the entertainment we consume: from books, to music, to video games, to sports. There's a reason Shakespeare wrote tragedies as well as comedies, a reason the blues are called the blues, and a reason thrillers are called thrillers. We choose what we read, watch, and listen to as a way of choosing how to feel.

You can use this to your benefit. Next time you want to shift your mood, ask:

## What could I watch (or read or listen to) that would put me in a better mood?

Choose something that will help you feel the way you want to feel. Too often, we do the opposite. We feel lousy so we seek entertainment to reinforce that feeling. There are valid reasons for doing this; if you recently broke up with someone, for example, you might choose to watch a tragic love story because it makes you feel you're not alone in your pain. On the other hand, you could choose to watch a movie that ends happily. It can give you a sense of hope you might not otherwise experience in the depths of your despair. Either way, it's your choice. You can choose what to watch, read, or listen to, and in that way choose what to feel.

*Magic Questions* can help you choose wisely. Next time you're feeling an emotion you'd rather not feel, ask yourself:

## What's the opposite of what I'm feeling?

When you come up with an answer you like, ask this follow up:

## What would that feel like?

### *Movement*

Movement is linked to emotion. When you change how you move you change how you feel. If you want to feel differently, move differently. Turn it into a question:

## How can I move differently right now?

Have fun with this. Be creative. Most importantly, move.

If you're sitting, stand up. If you're standing, move around. Try some stretches, or push-ups, or jumping jacks. Dance as if nobody's watching. Do whatever exercise your health and conditioning allow.

Breathing is one of the most effective ways to change what we're feeling. When we're trying to calm someone down, we often say, "Take a deep breath." There's a reason for that. Our bodies and minds are hardwired together. What we do with one affects the other.

For instance, next time you're with a child who's throwing a tantrum, try this experiment. Ask the child to look up at the ceiling and tell you what color it is. (Yep, that's like question you asked yourself above.) Whatever answer the child gives you, look up at the ceiling and ask this follow-up question: *Are you sure?* Watch what happens.

Keep this in mind next time you're throwing a tantrum. Our emotions are a function of what's going on in our body and mind. If we change what we're doing with either, we change how we feel.

## Daydream

If you've ever had a daydream or a fantasy, you know how powerful they can be. They allow us to try out new feelings and new experiences—or relive past ones. We can go places and do things that we might not otherwise be able to do, all without physical risk or expense. Emotionally, our daydreams and fantasies can transport us wherever we want to be. If you're in a bad place, that might be enough to feel better.

Think of daydreaming as a skill that empowers you to choose how you feel. No, you can't snap your fingers and jump from one strong emotion to another. But you can begin the journey by thinking about something else and imagining how it would feel. Before you know it, the stranglehold the negative emotion has on you will be weakened, and a new emotion becomes a possibility.

Here's a *Magic Question* that can help you develop this skill. Next time you're trying to move from a negative emotion to a positive one, imagine where you'd like to end up. With that in mind, ask yourself:

### If I could feel that now, what would it feel like?

Don't be afraid to give your imagination a little help. We experience the world in terms of our five senses: Vision, hearing, touch, smell, and taste. When you want to imagine something in all its glory, fill in these sensory blanks. The more detail you can imagine, the more you'll feel. Think of it as your own version of virtual-reality. You get to adjust everything: the location, characters, lighting, colors, sounds, weather, objects around you, tastes and smells, and the feeling of what you're touching.

Once you identify how you'd like to feel, and begun to imagine what it would feel like, here's a useful finishing question:

## What would help me feel that way?

And this:

## How would I begin that?

As you learn how to consciously choose what you feel, keep in mind that emotions serve us in ways we don't always understand. Grief is an example. It can help us remember how much we care for what we've lost. If we could erase the grief, would we want to?

Emotions are our most authentic selves. We've evolved to be thinking animals, but we're still animals. We're still of this Earth, and emotions are how we feel most grounded.

All of our emotions have their place, but sometimes they wear out their welcome. That's when it's time to move on and change the channel on the movie we're watching in our brain. We can do that by thinking differently, moving in new ways, choosing to watch another channel, and naturally, by asking *Magic Questions*.

5

# How can I change my habits?

*W*e face so many decisions each day that we have to rely on mental shortcuts to cope with them. Two of the most useful shortcuts are routines and habits.

Routines allow us to delegate our most common choices to subconscious processing, such as the steps we take to get ready for work in the morning. Each of those steps is something we choose to do, but when we flip the switch to automatic we don't have to make so many conscious decisions.

As useful as a routine can be, it's nothing more than a sequence of well-rehearsed choices, any one of which we can change. You'd be amazed how refreshing that can feel. Start with something simple, like this:

### What's a different way to get to work this morning?

Think about it. Capture a few answers.

It might seem like a small thing, but if you take a different route to work it will give you new sights and sounds to discover, and the opportunity to think new thoughts. Even if you work from home, you can get to your workspace via a different route than you usually would. Maybe you'll notice something you wouldn't normally notice and think thoughts you wouldn't normally think. If you take the subway, bus, or carpool, pay attention to where you're going instead of looking at your phone. Notice what you wouldn't normally notice. Then do it again the next day and see what you missed.

A small change in routine can open your mind to large possibilities. As a bonus, when you make different choices about the least important matters in life, you remind yourself you can make different choices about the most important ones as well.

One easy way to change your routine is to sample something new. For instance, you could ask yourself:

*What type of music do I rarely listen to?*

Capture a few answers. Try a new type of music at least once a week. Think of it as a safe way to step outside your comfort zone. You might not like what you try, or it might become a lifelong passion. You can do the same thing with any of these questions:

*What news channels do I rarely watch?*
*What websites do I rarely visit?*
*What kinds of food do I rarely eat?*

Sample something new each week. When you do, you return bite-sized chunks of your life to the realm of conscious choice, a skill that empowers you to make new choices in any area of your life.

## *Habits*

Habits are routines on steroids. Like routines, they're a useful way to delegate some of life's recurring choices to the unconscious mind. Unlike routines, habits can assume a life of their own. Before we know it, our habits are no longer working for us; we're working for them. These unconscious choices become so compelling that they begin to direct our conscious choices. That's what makes a habit so hard to break; it resists our effort to regain conscious control of our choices. The good news is that once we understand habits as nothing more than preprogrammed choices, we can reprogram them, like the stations on a car stereo.

One way to deal with a bad habit is to replace it with a good one. Easier said than done, perhaps, but entirely possible. If there's a habit you'd like to change, this question can get the wheels turning:

## What new choice could replace my old habit?

For example, let's say by habit you grab a bag of cookies in the evening when you're watching TV, but you've decided it would be better if you eat an apple instead. At first, choosing the apple might feel wrong because the old habit is still telling you what to do. But over time, if you keep choosing the apple instead of the cookies, it will become easier and easier to do. Sooner than you'd think, your new choice will turn into a new habit. At that point, choosing the cookies won't feel right. All you have to do is repeat your new choice until it becomes habit.

We saw this in action in Chapter 12, Book I *("How can I turn Magic Questions into a habit?")* where we saw how to turn *Magic Questions* into a habit in just thirty days. The same process can help you replace any bad habit with a good one. Decide what new choice you'd like to make and practice it every day for thirty days. If you miss a day, start over. In thirty days, you will have substituted your new choice for your old habit. [1]

The trick is to realize you can make your new choice even when you're in the gravitational pull of your old habit. If you feel the tug of the old habit, ask yourself:

## How do I choose my new habit right now?

Make this question part of your new habit so you ask it automatically every time your old habit tries to kick in.

Some habits are so deeply ingrained they can make you feel as if you have no choice but to give in. If that happens, try a conditional question like this one:

If I could make that new choice, how would I go about it?

Good habits can be a powerful tool to help you design the life you choose. Try this question to get started:

What would I like to turn into a habit?

Capture your answers. Reflect on them. Choose one and commit to the thirty-day process. You'll create a new habit, and before you know it you'll form one of the most useful habits of all: the habit of choice.

6

# How can I increase my energy?

*L*ife requires energy. Every step we take, every task we accomplish during the day, every text we send or photo we share, even brushing our teeth before we collapse into bed, all these require energy. Without energy we can become depressed, which drains our energy even more and creates a downward spiral.

Better to ask this question:

## How can I increase my energy?

Listen to your answers. Capture them and reflect.

If you feel your energy level dropping during the day, ask the question again. Ask it as often as you need it. You'd be surprised how much it can perk you up, like when a teacher calls on you in class. We wake up when we know someone is paying attention to us, even if it's us.

Here are some questions that help you discover how energy works in your life:

## What do I do that leaves me refreshed?

## What do I do that leaves me energized?

When you have a sense of what works for you, figure out what doesn't:

> *What do I do that leaves me drained?*
> *What do I do that leaves me deflated?*

Once you know what energizes you and what doesn't, you can organize your world around the former and avoid the latter. You may have to change your schedule, not to mention your thinking. You may have to create new habits. If you want more energy, it's worth it.

Here's a question that can help you figure out what to do next:

## How do I learn to have more energy?

Listen to your answers. Think of energy as a new skill and set about learning it. There's an entire industry that can help, from books, to podcasts, to webinars. One way to discover these resources is to perform an internet search with this question as your query.

### *Exercise*

I'm amazed how few of us understand the value of exercise, despite the overwhelming attention it receives from celebrities, health gurus, and the media. Whatever your starting place, you can feel better and more energized by moving your body in a healthy way, and turning it into a daily habit. Even a simple thing like taking a regular walk can boost your energy and enhance your sense of well being.

Here's a question to get started:

## What exercise would I enjoy doing?

Some people don't like exercise. Maybe it's because they haven't discovered an exercise they like, or they misunderstand the nature of exercise. You don't have to go to the gym and lift weights unless that's something you enjoy. You don't have to do aerobics. You don't have to run marathons or ride fifty miles a day on a bike. All you have to do is move. If you're sitting, stand. Move around. If you're healthy enough, take the stairs instead of the elevator.

And you can't beat walking. You can do it almost anywhere, any time, at any pace, for a block or ten miles; whatever works for you. Some exercise gurus would have you believe you have to reach an aerobic state to do yourself any good. That's not true. Any movement that doesn't hurt you helps you. If it makes you breathe harder, so much the better, but you'll benefit merely from walking from point A to point B—however fast you do it—and making it a regular part of your day.

There's a problem, though. Exercise takes time, and your schedule is probably full. That's why you need to consult the world's greatest problem solver, your brain:

## How can I work exercise into my daily routine?

Listen to your answers. Come up with a way to fit a few minutes of exercise into your busy schedule.

Some people prefer to exercise first thing in the morning, others at the end of the day, and others at lunch or during a coffee break. Whatever works for you, turn it into a habit so you don't feel right if you skip a day. Once you reach this point with any form of exercise, you'll have more energy, feel better, and enjoy better health. One note of caution: if it's been a while since you've exercised, consult your doctor before you start something new. You're not doing anyone a favor if you drop dead on the bike path.

### *Food*

Food is another topic on which we are inundated with information, but woefully ignorant about how it affects our energy level. Fortunately, you have at your disposal the world's greatest expert on how food feels in your body. Ask yourself:

## What foods give me energy?

And this:

### *What foods drain my energy?*

Listen to your body. Pay attention to how you react to foods.

I used to love a glass of orange juice in the morning, until one day when I didn't have juice I noticed how much more energized I felt later on. I tried an experiment for a few days: One day with orange juice, and the next day without. Sure enough, whenever I drank orange juice I went into an energy tailspin about an hour later. At the time, I didn't understand why, but I didn't have to. All I had to do was stop drinking orange juice, which made a big difference in both my energy level and my productivity. Later, when I did some research and learned about the glycemic load that various foods deliver to the body, it all made sense. But I didn't have to do any of that research to listen to what my body was telling me. Neither do you.

When you're ready to pay attention to what your body is telling you, ask yourself:

## How can I eat in a way that increases my energy?

Experiment until you have a sense of which foods energize you and which don't.

Too often we eat according to what others tell us is good for us. There's nothing wrong with listening to experts, but your body knows more about what works for you than any expert does.

Vary your diet and pay attention to your energy level. In particular, carbohydrates and sugar can cause dramatic swings in energy, but even that varies from person to person. Don't worry about advice from others, listen to your body. That's especially true when it comes to snacks. If you feel groggy after a Danish or a candy bar, try something else for your next snack.

Fruit is my preferred choice because it's chock-full of nutrients and fiber. In my body it produces high energy with a low glycemic load. I get the boost without the crash. Your body may react differently, and that's the body you need to listen to. Just ask:

### What snacks leave me feeling energized?

## *Habits*

Not everything that feels good is good for you. Many substances we ingest feel pleasant at first, but over time they drain our energy and damage our body. Especially in excess. When we're younger, we feel like we can get away with almost anything. But over time, the cumulative effect of ingesting even moderate amounts of poison can kill you.

When I say poison, I'm talking about the usual suspects: Smoking, vaping, alcohol, recreational pharmaceuticals, and sugar. Yes, sugar. These things steal your energy and eventually your health. If you're addicted to any of these things and want to get back in the driver's seat, seek professional help. If they're just bad habits rather than addictions, create new habits, the way we did in the previous chapter.

For instance, think of something you're ready to consume less of. Ask yourself:

### How can I reduce my consumption of____?

Listen to your answers. Capture them.

This question may at first draw a blank. Not because there's nothing there, but because you're so hooked on that substance you won't allow yourself to contemplate less of it. Your bad habit is fighting back. If you find yourself in this situation, ask the question differently:

If I wanted to reduce my consumption of ____, how would I go about it?

Listen, capture, and reflect. You'll be surprised what you come up with.

You might also ask yourself this question:

What can I have instead of ____?

Figure out something better for you, like fruit, perhaps, or exercise, and turn to that next time you crave what you're trying to cut back on. At first, it might feel like an unnatural act. That's okay. Keep doing it and it will become a new habit.

### *Attitude*

For all the platitudes we've heard about attitude, it's only a habit. If your habitual attitude drains your energy, create a new habit. Figure out what attitude you'd rather have:

What attitude will energize me?

Listen to your answers. You don't need to preach to yourself—just listen. Trust your gut.

Here's an intriguing variation on that question:

How can I think in a way that will increase my energy?

If your attitude is draining you, think about something that energizes you. Keep practicing it until it becomes a habit.

Here's another approach:

## What attitude would I like to have right now?

In Chapter 4, Book II *(How would I like to feel right now?)* we saw that we have a remarkable ability to choose how we feel by choosing what we think about.

With that in mind, try this question:

## What attitude would make me feel the way I want to feel?

When you've answered that question, try this one:

## What would that attitude feel like?

Go there. Let yourself feel this new attitude. You can always go back to your old attitude if you want, so there's no risk in trying a new one on for size.

Or try this variation. In any question about attitude, substitute the phrase "frame of mind" for the word "attitude." Like this:

## What frame of mind would I like to have right now?

You might come up with some new and interesting answers.

### *Workflow*

How and when we do things can have a dramatic effect on our level of energy. For instance, when I'm facing a distasteful task I tackle it first. By getting it out of the way I have more energy for whatever comes next. If I reverse the workflow and avoid the dreaded task, then I keep feeling stress until I get around to it. Getting the unpleasant task out of the way gives me energy and peace of mind for the rest of the day, and it gives me something to look forward to instead of something to dread.

Another way to increase your energy is to get organized. When we put away what doesn't need to be in front of us, we're free to focus on what does.

Getting organized applies to our workspace, but it also applies to how we work. For example, if it takes several steps to finish a task you perform often, ask yourself:

## How can I do this in fewer steps?

Or:

## What's a better way to do this?

Let your brain work on the problem for a minute or two. Listen to your answers and capture them.

Sometimes you need a better tool to improve your workflow, like a ratchet screwdriver instead of an old-fashioned one. Or a macro program for your computer or phone, one that compresses several steps into a single command. Or maybe you need to learn a new skill that can help you get more done in less time.

You can turn these needs into *Magic Questions*:

## What tool could help me improve my workflow?

And this:

## What new skill could help me improve my workflow?

For example, most cell phones, tablets, and computers have decent voice recognition, but most people don't use it. There's a learning curve to adapt your brain to the eccentricities of dictating and issuing commands by voice, but it's worth the price of admission. You'll save time, reduce the potential for repetitive-motion injuries, and wonder why you didn't take advantage of this remarkable technology a long time ago.

You can improve workflow for everything you do. From your job, to your hobbies, to washing the dishes, there's a way of doing things that will help you feel more energized and be more productive.

Here are some questions to figure out what's best for you:

How can I organize my workspace to better support my work?

How can I organize my day to better support my work?

What workflow might make me feel more productive?

One of life's greatest stressors is to feel that our world is beyond our control. Improving workflow can help us regain a sense of control. The result is we feel less stress, more energy, and more satisfaction in what we do.

You can even turn it into a question:

How can I control more of my day?

Little changes can pay large emotional dividends.

### Sleep

Sleep is the single most important factor in our level of energy. How we manage the other factors deeply affects our sleep; in turn, they are deeply affected by our sleep. If we aren't optimizing the areas above, then we probably aren't sleeping as well as we might. If we aren't sleeping well, then we probably aren't optimizing the areas above.

Improving our sleep is often more challenging than improving other energy factors. When it comes to them, we can buckle down and work harder. But how do we buckle down with sleep? Even worse, when we're busy we tend to treat sleep as a necessary evil, something we have to do at the end of the day when we run out of time and energy for more productive activities.

The opposite is true. Getting better sleep is the most productive thing we can do. When we maximize our sleep potential, not only do we feel better and healthier, but we increase the amount of energy and productive time we can devote to other activities.

Sleep potential deals with more than the time we spend sleeping; it's about the quality of our sleep. Each of us has an ideal way of sleeping that will maximize the health and energy benefits of sleep. Since that varies so much from one person to the next, even expert advice about sleep can provide only general guidance. It's up to us to figure out the best approach.

There are many resources to help you learn how to sleep better, but you might as well start with the most important expert of all. Ask yourself:

## How can I sleep better?

And this:

## How can I awaken more refreshed?

Listen to your answers. Chances are you already know how to sleep better than you do.

For instance, maybe you shouldn't binge watch your favorite thriller right before bedtime, or eat chocolate cake while you do, or have that extra cup of coffee in the afternoon. Maybe you should exercise today instead of putting it off until tomorrow. Maybe you should get a new mattress or take a meditation class. Maybe the alerts on your cell phone keep waking you up at the most inopportune times. Maybe the blinds on your window don't do a good job of blocking out the streetlight next-door. Maybe your partner's snoring doesn't help.

Each of these things can be fixed, or at least improved. To a great extent, restful sleep is about doing a good job of managing your sleeping environment. With a little thought and effort, there isn't much about that environment you can't improve if you choose to do so.

Turn it into a *Magic Question*:

## How can I improve my sleeping environment?

Brainstorm. Listen to your answers and reflect on them. You don't have to fix everything at once; pick something and start there

You can also ask a useful follow-up question

## If I wanted to sleep better, what would I do?

With each change you make, see how energized you feel when you wake up in the morning and as you progress through the day.

Research can help, so feel free to ask yourself:

## How can I learn to sleep better?

When you've heard your answers to this question, turn it into an internet search.

You can also seek medical advice, but you might want to try some of the easier fixes first. Figure out how to have less light in the room, less noise, and a more consistent routine for when you go to bed and get up. You can make good sleep a habit like any other habit, with practice.

Make sure there's no cell phone where you can hear it. For those of us addicted to our phones, that's hard, but interruptions destroy restful sleep. If you think sleep is more important than interruptions, get rid of the interruptions.

When you improve your sleep, you'll increase your potential in every other area of your life, and feel more energy than you ever thought possible.

## 7

## How can I relax?

*S*tress is the great sinkhole of energy and emotion. When we come face-to-face with adverse or demanding circumstances, our reptilian brain tends to shift into fight-or-flight mode. If neither is an option, which is most of the time in our contemporary world, then our emotions tend to implode. Depending on the circumstances, we react in different ways. Sometimes we feel hyper. Sometimes we feel drained. Sometimes we feel both at the same time, which is truly disorienting. The greater the stress, the greater the mood swing—and the energy swing.

There are two ways to deal with stress: Change what's causing it, or change how we feel about it.

Start with the obvious question:

### What makes me feel stress?

Listen and capture. The more sources of stress you uncover, the better you'll be able to deal with them.

Here's the next question:

### How can I relax?

Listen, capture, and reflect. This is a broad question, but don't be surprised if you come up with specific answers.

Here's a variation:

### How can I reduce my stress?

Here's a "What if?" version:

### If I wanted to reduce my stress, how would I go about it?

Your answers to these questions provide insight into what's causing you stress, as well as ideas about how to reduce it. Treat each question like a brainstorming session: the more ideas the better. Along the way, you might be surprised at how large an impact you can have by making a small change.

Suppose, for example, that one of the stressors you identify is the person sitting in the cubicle next to you. They're so loud you feel drained at the end of the day. Ask yourself:

### How can I sit in a different location?

There may be several options available to you. Maybe you can move to another team, or another room, or another geographic location. Maybe you can work from home. Whatever sounds right to you, imagine yourself working from that new location and ask:

### How would I feel if I could make that change?

If you experience an overwhelming sense of relief, then it's probably worth doing something about it. If it doesn't make much difference, maybe something else is behind your stress.

If you can't change what's causing you stress, or choose not to, then change how you feel about it. Think of something that's causing you stress and ask:

## What if that didn't stress me out?

Or this:

## How would I feel if that didn't stress me out?

The dirty little secret about stress is that it doesn't come from without; it comes from within. When you feel stressed about something, those feelings are coming from you, not from the situation. The loud person in the next cubicle isn't causing you stress—your reaction is.

Stress comes from how we interpret circumstances. Think of the difference between riding a roller coaster and falling off a building. The core experiences may be similar, but we define them quite differently.

If that's hard to accept, consider this. We all know people who seem to feel no stress at all in situations that would cause us considerable anxiety. How does a musician perform in front of a huge audience without missing a note? How does a basketball player sink a foul shot with the championship on the line? How does a kindergarten teacher handle a room full of five-year-olds? How does a waiter handle ten tables at once without going stark raving mad?

It's not that they don't feel stress; they've learned how to deal with stress in those situations. They've prepared their minds and bodies to handle what would create stress for the rest of us. Yet if you placed them in unfamiliar circumstances they would feel as much stress as the next person. Could the basketball player wait tables in a busy restaurant? Could the kindergarten teacher perform before a packed concert hall? Could the musician handle those five-year-olds?

Whatever circumstances induce stress in you, you can choose to think differently about them by asking different questions.

What stresses me about this and how can I change it?

How would I feel if I weren't stressed?

What would it feel like to have no stress?

How would someone else feel who doesn't get stressed in this situation?

In many cases, stress is only fear talking. Maybe you feel stress in performance reviews because you're afraid of criticism. Maybe you're afraid to meet new people, so you feel stress when you do. Maybe you're afraid to leave your comfort zone so you feel stress whenever you venture beyond it. We touched on the subject of fear in Chapter 11, Book I *(What am I afraid of?)* For now, here are some questions that can help you deal with underlying fears:

What am I afraid of?

The first step in managing fear is to identify it. Fears aren't quite as scary in broad daylight.

Then you can ask:

What if I weren't afraid of that?

Or this:

How would it feel if I weren't afraid?

Here's one of my favorites:

What if I allowed myself to enjoy the situation?

Some circumstances are always stressful. When you encounter those, or you're about to, you can reduce your stress if you prepare for it. Here are some questions that can help:

How would I feel if I were prepared for this?

What kind of preparation might free me from stress?

How can I be better prepared for this?

How can I prepare my body and mind for what I'm about to do?

The better prepared we are to deal with what the world throws at us, the less we'll suffer from stress.

# 8

# What is my opinion?

*F*rom social media, to pundits, to the loudmouth in the room, we're inundated with the opinions of others. With so much noise it's easy to adopt an opinion from someone else and treat it as our own. Entire industries exist to help us do precisely that. From business, to politics, to religion, vested interests would like nothing better than to have us think what they tell us to think.

If you prefer to think for yourself, consider one of your strongly held opinions. It might be about politics, religion, brand loyalty, fashion, sports, you name it. Write that opinion down. Then ask yourself:

## What do I really know about that?

Listen to your answers. Capture them. Give yourself as much time as you need.

You might know a lot, or you might know a little. Either way, it's useful to get it out in the open so you have an idea of what's behind your opinion.

Now comes the fun part. With the same opinion in mind, ask:

## What don't I know about that?

Again, capture whatever you have to say. Give yourself time for this; what you don't know is likely to be far more than what you do.

Take religion, for example. By one estimate there are 4,200 active religions in the world.[1] If you subscribe to any one of them, what do you know about the others? Opinions about religion are among our most cherished. Yet whatever we believe, the majority of our fellow human beings believe something else, and we know next to nothing about what that is or why. Despite that, we tend to feel certain that we're right and they're wrong, or at least they're ignorant about the version of truth we subscribe to.

Opinions about religion may be the most dramatic example, but the same logic holds for everything else we believe. Consider the strongly held opinion you identified above. Whatever it is, billions of people disagree with you. They're as certain that opinion is wrong as you're certain it's right. Let that sink in for a moment, and ask yourself:

## What do they know that I don't?

Take as long as you want to listen to your answers. The people who disagree with you have reasons for what they believe, just as you do. Who knows what you might learn from them if you give yourself a chance?

The idea isn't to embarrass ourselves with our own ignorance. Like it or not, we're going to form opinions about things we know little or nothing about. That's human nature. We're going to cling to those opinions as if our lives depended on it. That's also human nature. But are they actually our opinions, or are they spoon fed to us by someone else, for their benefit rather than ours?

Socrates taught us that the unexamined life is not worth living.[2] That's a lot to ponder, so let's pare it down into something more digestible: *The unexamined opinion is not worth having.*

The next time someone offers you their opinion on a matter of importance, ask yourself:

What is my opinion about that?

Then ask this follow-up question:

What do I really think about that?

Ask the other questions above as additional follow-up questions.

If we don't examine our opinions we'll never get to know ourselves. We've been taught to have the courage of our convictions, but are they our convictions or those of someone else? Give yourself the opportunity to find out. As the poet famously said:

> *Who knows what you'll learn about you*
> *When you examine an opinion or two?*

Okay, that was me, but you get the point.

# 9

## How can I design my own life?

*W*e live our lives partly by design and partly by default. To live by default means we react. Whatever the world gives us, we react the way the world has taught us to react. To live by design is the opposite. Whatever the world gives us, we pause from our reactions long enough to make our own choices.

Consider something you do because you think you have no choice. It can involve anything: a relationship, your career, or whatever you're supposed to do next weekend. Ask yourself:

### If it were up to me, what choice would I make?

Two things happen when you ask this question. First, you pause from reacting long enough to give yourself a chance to think. Second, you remind yourself that it's up to you. It's always been up to you. Like Dorothy in the Wizard of Oz, you've had this power all along, though you might not have realized it.

Whatever your internal programming, wherever it came from, that's all history now. Whatever has gotten you to this point belongs to your past. All that matters now is what you choose to do in the present. Not because the past is meaningless, but because it's unreachable, untouchable, and unchangeable.

The present is another story. From this point forward, you have the power to choose what you do with every moment as it comes. Welcome home, Dorothy.

You can start with one of the most important questions there is:

## How can I design my own life?

When we're children, we're taught how to behave. As we grow older, we're given increasing responsibility to make our own choices. Yet the world continues to program us with the choices it wants us to make. We're taught about free will, but we're discouraged from exercising it. Instead, our parents and teachers want us to do what they tell us to do. Businesses want us to buy their products. Employers want us to do our jobs the way they require it. Religions want us to believe what they tell us to believe. Politicians want us to vote for them.

All these people are coming from their point of view, not yours. It's possible they want what's best for you. But they definitely want what's best for them. Not because they have ulterior motives—although some may—but all they can truly know is what's best for them. The only point of view any of us can experience authentically is our own. When we try to put ourselves in someone else's place, the best we can manage is to do so from our point of view.

Other people don't have a clue what's best for you, no matter how loudly they insist they do. Only you can decide. You can listen to all of their advice, some of it, or none of it. What you choose to do is entirely up to you.

Once you understand that, you can begin to live your life by design rather than by default. You can choose to act, rather than to react.

Here's a question that can get you started:

## What life would I design for myself?

Listen to what you have to say. No one else on Earth can answer this question for you. Capture your answers. Keep them in the present tense or imagine the future. The past is past, beyond any power to change.

Consider your answers. Whatever they are, here's a follow-up question:

## How can I design that life for myself?

Again, listen to yourself and jot down your answers.

After you've taken a minute or two to reflect on them, ask this:

## What advice would I give to someone who wanted to design that life for themselves?

Sometimes it's easier to listen to our own advice when we think we're giving it to someone else.

Here's a follow-up:

## How would it feel to live that life?

Reflect on your answers. Then ask the now-familiar question that makes everything else possible:

## What am I going to do about it?

You now have all the ammunition you need to answer this question. The chapters to come will improve your aim.

# Part 2: Magic in Action

# 10

# Where do I begin?

$\mathcal{G}$ ood questions open the door to good answers. But even with good answers, you still have to do something with them. When you come up with a great idea, you still have to put it into action.

Consider changes you'd like to make in your life and settle on one to tackle first. Turn it into a question:

## What is the first thing I would change in my life?

You've already been over this more than once, so go with the first thought that pops in your head. With that in mind, ask yourself:

## Where do I begin?

Listen to your answers and capture them.

If it's a big project, you might come up with a series of steps. Prioritize them in terms of which step to do first. When you've settled on one, begin with it—right now, before you do anything else. If it's a significant step, break it into smaller steps, until you come up with one you can do immediately. Then do it.

If it helps, turn it into a question:

## What step can I take before I leave this room?

Whatever you come up with, take action now. That's how you begin.

### *Inertia*

Inertia is a law of physics. A body at rest tends to stay at rest unless acted upon by an external force. A body in motion tends to stay in motion unless acted upon by an external force.

Something similar applies with human behavior. You're a body at rest until you decide to set yourself in motion, and vice versa. This psychological inertia is every bit as immutable as physical inertia. No wonder it's so easy for us to get stuck.

But there's an important difference. With physical inertia, a body remains at rest or in motion until acted upon by an external force. With psychological inertia, the force can come from within us. We can choose to become a body in motion or remain a body at rest.

That's why it's so important to begin right here, right now. Whatever first step you've identified to create the change you want to make in your life, begin that step now. Turn yourself into a body in motion. Momentum will help you stay that way. That's how to make inertia work for you.

The alternative is procrastination. That's how to make inertia work against you. It's so easy to remain a body at rest by putting something off until tomorrow that tomorrow never comes.

If you procrastinate, here's a question that can help you use procrastination to your advantage:

## How can I put off procrastinating?

Once you finish the first step you've identified above, and you're a body in motion, you can ask one of the world's most useful questions:

## What do I do next?

Then do it. Turn your thought into action. As important as good ideas are, they're only theory. Change won't happen until you put that theory into practice. You become a body in motion when you take action.

For instance, suppose the change you've decided to make is getting in shape. That's a wonderful objective because it affects so much else in your life, from your energy, to your self-confidence. But depending on what condition you're in, it may be a significant project that consists of many smaller steps. To identify what those steps might be, you can ask yourself:

## How do I get in shape?

Ultimately, you'll want to create a plan of action to take you from where you are to where you want to be. But for now, the trick is to get started. You need to identify one step you can begin before leaving this room and then do it. You might do some stretching exercises, if you're physically capable of doing so, or read a chapter or two in that book about nutrition you've been meaning to read, or search the web for advice about how to get in shape. Each of these actions will turn you from a body at rest into a body in motion. Momentum will help you stay in motion.

One of the basic principles of planning is to begin with the end in mind. Maybe there's a certain weight you'd like to obtain, or a dress size or waist size you're shooting for, or an endurance goal you'd like to achieve. You can figure it out in advance with a question like this:

What am I trying to accomplish?

And this

How will I know when I'm done?

And this

What will success look like?

Here's another useful question:

What new habits will help me keep my momentum?

Once you're a body in motion, you want to stay in motion until you reach your objective. Habits are a great way to do that.

Whatever change you've decided to make in your life, begin it now. Begin with your end in mind. Identify an action you can take before you leave this room and do it. Enjoy the elation of becoming a body in motion, and the pleasure of remaining in motion until you get what you want.

# 11

# How do I finish?

*Y*ears ago, I attended a training session on how we communicate with ourselves about fears and limitations. One of the exercises was to climb a telephone pole, stand on top, and jump to a trapeze. Having recently seen the movie *Karate Kid*, I decided to increase the degree of difficulty. I visualized myself climbing to the top of the pole, standing on one leg in the "crane" position, and executing the snap kick like the kid in the movie.

When it was my turn, I climbed the rungs, stood on top of a telephone pole thirty-five feet above the California desert, slowly raised my leg just like in the movie, and executed the kick I had so carefully visualized. I felt like I was on top of the world.

Exhilarated, I leaped to the trapeze, and felt my body swing out into space with what instantly became an unbearable weight. My hands were ripped from the bar and I fell.

We all wore a safety harness, so falling was no big deal. But failing was, at least for me, and I felt like I'd failed. I had planned for everything except the finish. It never occurred to me that the force of gravity would require me to grip the bar so tightly.

As they lowered me to the ground, I wondered:

## What can I learn from this?

The answer was as obvious as it was profound: *Plan your finish.* That lesson has served me well ever since.

Consider something you have to do that will test you in unanticipated ways. With this in mind, ask yourself:

## How do I finish?

Think it through. With your finish in mind, ask:

## What will it feel like?

Allow yourself to experience the feeling in advance. Then ask:

## What is likely to be the greatest challenge?

With that in mind, ask:

## How will I prepare for this challenge?

If you believe, as I do, that much of luck is what happens when preparation meets opportunity, you'll do yourself a favor and ask questions that help you prepare not just to begin, but to finish as well.

# 12

## How do I learn that?

*W*hen we come into this world, our full-time job is to learn. We have to learn how to talk, walk, read, write, do math, interact with our fellow human beings, and a thousand other things along the way. These accomplishments seem so remarkable at such an early age they give rise to the myth that we have a greater capacity to learn as children than we do as adults.

The opposite is true. Children are a blank slate. They start from scratch so they have no choice but to learn. Adults do. We can choose to learn or not. If we choose to learn, our knowledge and experience give us a greater capacity to learn than we had as children. The more we learn, the more we can learn.

However, we do face a challenge as adults we didn't face as kids. We don't just have to learn—we have to unlearn. New knowledge often comes at the expense of existing knowledge, which is deeply entrenched in our memory. New skills frequently require the unlearning of old skills. This can be intimidating, especially for people who fear change.

But change is here whether we like it or not. According to a recent study, the half-life of a job skill today is about five years.[1] That means if you want to hold on to your job that long, you're going to have to learn a bunch of new skills and update old ones just to keep up with changes in the workplace. That's a daunting prospect, especially if you've convinced yourself you can't learn. If you have, that's the first thing you have to unlearn.

This question can help:

## How can I unlearn that?

As adults we can learn anything we put our mind to, at any age. We're lucky enough to live in a golden age of learning. All we have to do is consult our virtual BFFs: Google, Alexa, and Siri. Want to know the annual rainfall in Patagonia? Somewhere between 200 and 400 mm a year, according to Alexa. That answer took all of three seconds. Want a degree in meteorology? Google tells me how I can earn a degree online, or where I can study at brick-and-mortar campuses across the country. Want to catch up on the latest research on climate change? Siri points me to dozens of resources, from news outlets to academic journals. We can also ask our human friends, including our extended family of friends on social media sites that span the globe. Beyond these ad hoc resources there are many online providers of high-quality learning in any subject you can imagine.

Whatever you want to learn, it's easier today than ever before, which is fortunate because as change accelerates our need to learn accelerates.

You can get the ball rolling with this question:

## What do I want to learn?

Listen to your answers. Give yourself a minute or two. Capture and reflect on them. Then ask this follow-up question:

## If I could learn one new skill, what would it be?

Let your imagination have fun. Capture whatever pops into your mind. Maybe there's a new skill you need to acquire for work, or a new app to master on your phone. Maybe you'd like to learn how to cook a dish you tried at a local restaurant, or manage your finances, or repair a leaky faucet, or learn how to play a guitar. Settle on something you'd like to learn, and ask yourself:

## How do I learn that?

By now you've learned the drill. Listen to your answers. Capture them. Reflect. Spend a moment to put together a list of steps to learn whatever it is you want to learn.

Today's learning resources are so remarkable all we have to do is ask a question of the internet, like this:

## How do I _____?

Fill in the blank with whatever you want to learn how to do, such as repair a toaster, cook prime rib, or learn calculus.

For example, I've been a photographer since I was six. Recently I invested in a new camera optimized to take pictures of birds in flight. That's one of my favorite subjects, as you can see from the photos I've posted on *KeithEllis.com*. As sophisticated as the new camera was, the documentation that came with it was a joke. I had a choice: figure out how to use it on my own or learn from someone who already had.

I decided to put a question to the internet:

*How do I take pictures of birds in flight with the [make and model] camera?*

Seconds later I was viewing a video posted by a professional photographer who demonstrated exactly what I wanted to do with my new camera. I would have paid to watch his tutorial, but it didn't cost me a dime. I did buy one of his books because I like to support people who support me. A few hours later I was taking pictures I could have only dreamed about the day before.

Some people are intimidated by learning something new or unlearning something old. If that describes you, ask yourself:

## How can I fall in love with learning again?

We're born to learn. When we were kids, learning was fun. It was all about exploration and discovery. Then we were plopped down in a chair in a classroom and told to pay attention. What had been fun began to feel tedious and boring. Even then, a quality teacher could inspire us to learn. The good news is that with all the resources available online today, excellent teachers and the joy of learning are only a few clicks away.

Think of something you need to learn, and ask yourself:

## What if I could learn that?

Give yourself a minute or two to consider it, and ask this follow-up question:

## If I could learn it, how would I go about it?

Capture some answers, and ask yourself:

## If I did learn it, how would I feel?

In the golden age of learning, we have a golden opportunity to be lifelong learners—but only if we allow ourselves.

# 13

# What motivates me?

*M*otivation is a tricky thing. Sometimes we need a carrot; other times a stick. Sometimes we need both. To make it even more interesting, our motivation can change with context. What motivates us to get out of bed in the morning might not motivate us to do our taxes, just as what motivates us to learn a new video game might not inspire us to learn a new language. What motivates us when we're in a good mood won't necessarily motivate us when we're in a lousy one.

Think of something you want to change in your life. With this in mind, ask yourself:

## What would motivate me to do that?

Capture whatever pops into your mind. If you have all the motivation you need for this objective, then consider a different one, and ask the same question.

When you're finished, ask this variation:

## What would make this change worthwhile?

Your answers to these questions tell you something useful about yourself. Not only about what motivates you, but about how badly you want to be motivated. Not all change is worth the effort. To see something through to the end you not only have to commit, but it has to be worth it. Otherwise, there's no reason to follow through.

With the same objective for change in mind, ask this:

## What makes this worth doing?

The greater the difficulty of the change you have in mind, the more certain you need to be that it's worth it. I'd love to play lead guitar in a rock band, but not enough to practice eight hours a day, give up everything else I could be doing during that time, and spend my life on the road. Even if I had the talent, it wouldn't be worth it.

Here's a question that will help you understand the kind of commitment you're asking yourself to make:

## What price will I have to pay to make this change?

When you've tackled that, ask this follow up question:

## What will I have to give up to make that change?

To get what we want from life, we often have to give up something we want less. The better we understand this trade off, the more clearly we can understand the commitment it requires.

Here's a question that can help:

## What will I have to sacrifice to make this change?

### Opportunity Cost

If you've ever taken a class in economics, you've encountered the notion of *opportunity cost*. The time and money you commit to one course of action is no longer available for any other course of action. The true cost of one action includes the cost of not doing others.

For instance, if you choose to go to a movie on Saturday night, then you're giving up all the other things you might have done, such as going to a party, a ballgame, a concert, or spending a quiet evening at home.

Every choice we make comes with an opportunity cost, whether we're aware of it or not. If we choose to invest time and resources in one activity, then we're choosing not to invest those in any other activity. Our choices have consequences not only from what we do, but from what we choose not to do. If you want to see something through, it's good to understand your opportunity cost going in.

This question can help:

### What is my opportunity cost for doing this?

Once you have a clear sense of what making a change will cost you in terms of time, resources, sacrifice, and opportunity cost, then you're in a position to ask:

### Is this change worth the price to me?

If it is, you're all set. If it's not, then focus on what is.

Motivation is not about tricking yourself into working harder, it's about knowing yourself. It's about knowing what's required of you to get where you want to go, and whether you're willing to undertake that much heavy lifting to get there. If you are, your motivation will take care of itself.

### *Intrinsic Value*

Ask yourself:

## What do I genuinely enjoy doing?

Take at least a couple of minutes for this one. Give your mind the freedom to roam.

When you're done, look at the things you have to do, the price you have to pay, to make the change you decided to make above. Notice anything?

There's a difference between doing something because you enjoy it, and doing something because it leads to something else. The former is intrinsically valuable. You do it because it feels good. It's an end in itself. The latter is extrinsically valuable. It's a means to an end, not an end in itself. You do it not because you want the experience, but because you want the results.

When we're working to make a meaningful change in our lives, we spend a lot of time doing extrinsically valuable tasks. We aren't doing them because we enjoy them; we're doing them because they lead to something else. They aren't ends in themselves—they're means to an end. Imagine how much easier it would be if some of those means to an end included things you enjoy doing.

One way to motivate yourself is to incorporate intrinsically valuable activities into your extrinsically valuable tasks. The more you can incorporate what you like to do in what you have to do, the more motivated you'll be to do it.

You can turn it into a question:

## How can I include more of what I enjoy doing in what I have to do?

For instance, I've spent most of my adult life in front of a computer. Through the years I've devoted so much time to pointing, clicking, and waiting for something to happen that I finally realized I could make my workday more enjoyable and more productive if I invested in a faster computer. At the time, the computer I had worked fine. The frugal part of my brain told the fun-loving part of my brain that it would be a waste of money to get a new computer. But I threw financial caution to the wind, and bought the fastest computer I could find, with the nicest screen.

What a difference! I couldn't wait to start work in the morning. I was already lucky enough to be doing what that I loved, but I found myself loving it even more. I spent more time working because it felt less like work. I added an extra hour of productivity to every day, not because I forced myself to, but because it felt like play. I was able to spend more of my workday enjoying what I was doing. As a bonus, the extra work paid for the new computer in a matter of weeks.

Along those lines, here's a question you might find useful:

## What can I do that would help me enjoy my work more?

In my example, the sheer joy of driving a faster computer motivated me to work more.

What motivates you? You're the only one who can answer that. You're the only one who knows what makes you tick.

Here's a question that can help you figure it out:

## What do I look forward to?

Here's a useful follow-up:

## What gets me excited?

Whatever your answers are to these questions, the more of it you can inject into your work, the less it will feel like work.

### *Incentives*

If you've ever received a performance-based incentive at work, you understand how powerful it can be. Why not use the same psychology on yourself?

Go back to the change you identified at the beginning of this chapter. Presumably, the ultimate payoff is worth the price. But if it's a demanding project or involves doing things you don't like doing, it can't hurt to sweeten the pot.

## What incentive can I offer myself to do that?

Think of incentives as a reward for doing what you commit to doing. But make sure you don't offer yourself incentives that cause you to backslide. For example, if you're trying to lose ten pounds during the next two months, it doesn't make sense to reward yourself with a chocolate sundae when you reach your goal. Instead, a new outfit or a new toy might be a good idea—or a day off where you do nothing but what you enjoy. Imagine a whole day filled with activities that are ends in themselves.

You'll get the most bang for your buck if you pick an incentive that contributes to your objective. Suppose, for instance, that your objective is to increase endurance in your exercise of choice. One incentive you could offer yourself when you reach a specific milestone is to get some new exercise equipment, or upgrade your gym membership, or invest in a new watch that automatically measures your heartbeat. Not only will it give you a little extra incentive to reach your initial milestone, but it will serve as a tool to help you accomplish the next milestone. It's like earning compound interest on motivation.

14

## What do I risk if I don't try?

*N*o one likes to fail, although failing is how we've accomplished most of what we've done in life. When we were youngsters we didn't just start walking; we had to fall down a lot until we got it right. We didn't just start talking; we had to learn how to speak poorly before we could speak well. We didn't just start reading; we began by misreading and mispronouncing until we learned how to do it right. This process of trial and error is what made us who we are. It can also make us who we want to be, as long as we're willing to keep trying new things, and keep learning from our mistakes.

Yet some people dread failure so much they refuse to risk it. They settle into a comfort zone where there's no trial and error, no learning, and no growth. They think they're avoiding risk, but all they're avoiding is life.

There's a better way. Learn to take reasonable risks. This starts by asking reasonable questions.

Suppose, for example, that you want a promotion. You might ask yourself:

## What are the risks of pursuing that?

One obvious risk is that you might fail to get the promotion. If that bothers you, ask:

## Is it worth the risk?

If your answer is yes, then it would be reasonable to take the risk. If your answer is no, then ask this now-familiar question:

## What am I afraid of?

Listen to yourself and capture your answers. It's hard to break out of your comfort zone if you have no idea what's keeping you there, so it helps to get it out in the open.

Some people are afraid of success. In our example above, if you get a promotion it might mean you have to work longer hours. You might have to learn new skills, or speak more often in front of a group. You might have to relocate. You might even have to update your self-image to accommodate the new, more successful you.

For each fear you uncover, ask yourself:

## Is the promotion worth that risk?

If it is, move on to the next fear. If it's not worth the risk, then ask a follow-up question that can help you get to the bottom of things:

## What am I really afraid of?

Fears often masquerade as something else: An obstacle that seems too large to overcome, a sacrifice that seems too great, or a violation of a personal standard we've assumed for ourselves. But beneath the surface is good old-fashioned fear.

When we face our fear in the light of day, acknowledge it, intelligently evaluate the risk, and commit to taking the risk despite our fear, then we feel unstoppable, even if we're still afraid. Courage isn't the absence of fear, it's doing what we're afraid of.

When we evaluate the risk of doing something, we often ignore one of the most important factors of all:

## What do I risk if I don't try?

In the previous chapter, we considered the opportunity cost of making a choice. We should also consider the opportunity cost of not making that choice. When we're deciding whether to do something or not, we owe it to ourselves to understand the true cost of both.

In our "promotion" example above, if all we evaluate is the risk of going after the promotion, it's only half the story. Here's a question for the other half:

## What's the risk of not going after the promotion?

This question might lead to others that fill in important blanks, such as:

What's the risk of losing that extra income?

What's the risk to my career if I don't move up that next rung on the ladder?

What's the risk if I don't get to work with the people I might have worked with?

What's the risk if I don't allow myself to stretch and grow in this new direction?

What's the risk if I don't add this to my resume?

When you evaluate the risk of making a meaningful change in your life, do yourself a favor and also consider the risks of not doing it. It may not change your mind, but at least you'll understand what you're missing. Then the choice belongs to you, rather than to fear lurking in the darkness.

## 15

# What will I wish I had done differently?

*I*n *A Christmas Carol,* by Charles Dickens, Scrooge was haunted by three ghosts, but the one that really shook him up was "The Ghost of Christmas Yet to Come." Scrooge took one look at what the future had in store for him and changed.

We can learn from his lesson. We can't change the past, but we can change the future by what we do right now. We can take a long hard look at where we're going, and if we don't like what we see, we can make changes today that will change our tomorrows.

Here's a question that can help:

Tomorrow, what will I wish I'd done yesterday?

Capture your thoughts and give yourself time to reflect on them.

When you're finished, here's a more pointed version:

Tomorrow, what will I regret having done today?

Or look at the other side of the coin:

Tomorrow, what will I regret not having done today?

Shift the timeframe by asking:

Next year, what will I regret having done this year?

And this:

Next year, what will I regret not having done this year?

Regret is a powerful emotion. Why not put it to good use?

Now imagine yourself twenty years in the future, looking back on this part of your life. Ask yourself:

What do I wish I'd done differently?

Spend some time with this. Listen to yourself and reflect. Whatever your imaginary future may hold, it's not too late to change it by making different choices now.

### Ellis's Law

When I was in second grade, my teacher tried to help us understand the value of compound interest. The first step was to put our pennies into a savings account. Like most kids, I prefered to invest my pennies in candy and ice cream, where they belonged. Predictably, years later I did the math and realized how much money I would've had if only I'd listened to what Mrs. Miller had tried to teach me.

The more I thought about it, the more fascinated I became with the principle of compounding, not only for how it affected money, but how it seemed to touch everything in life. Compounding is how we make time work for us instead of against us. It may not seem like a magic bullet, but it's the closest thing I've found.

When we take action every day, even something small, over time these efforts compound themselves. Results accumulate by building on prior results. This notion eventually became what I call *Ellis's Law*:

*Over time, even ordinary efforts yield extraordinary results.*

I don't call it *Ellis's Law* because I created it, but because it created me. When I finally understood the implications, it changed my life.

*Ellis's Law* applies to everything we do. Given enough time, even our smallest actions can become significant. Anyone who has gained weight can attest to that. Nobody sets out to add inches to their waistline or hips. But a glass of wine here, a hot fudge sundae there, and before you know it, you've produced an extraordinary result that stares back at you in the mirror. You might not like what you see, but it's proof positive that even small efforts, over time, produce big results. Once you understand that, you can begin to make time work for you instead of against you.

## 16

## What could go right?

*F*or many of us, when we face something new or challenging, our first thoughts are about what could go wrong. That's a valid concern. If you're learning to skateboard, it's not unreasonable to think about falling, which you undoubtedly will do. But it's equally valid—and far more useful—to focus on what could go right.

When we imagine doing something, we tend to do what we're visualizing because the brain is wired that way. When we imagine what we don't want to happen, we're unintentionally giving our brain instructions to make it happen. We're far more likely to succeed if we think about succeeding then we are if we think about what could go wrong.

Consider something you're worried about doing. Maybe it's taking a test, or speaking in front of a group, or asking someone out. Instead of thinking about everything that could go wrong, ask yourself:

## What could go right?

Let yourself imagine that. Allow yourself to dwell on it for a minute or two. Congratulations, you've just increased your odds for success.

Take public speaking, for example. Many people fear it. They can't stop thinking about what could go wrong. They're afraid they might make a fool out of themselves, or forget what they're supposed to say, or step off the podium in the wrong direction and fall down. Okay, maybe that last one is just me. I actually did that once—in church.

When you're preparing to speak in front of a group, whatever you're afraid might happen might actually happen. Or might not. You get to choose which set of possibilities to focus on. No matter which outcome you visualize, you increase the chances it will occur.

No wonder so many athletes practice visualization. Basketball players shoot thousands of foul shots in practice, but they also practice in their mind's eye by visualizing successful foul shots. They do it when they're not on the court and when they are; visualizing a successful shot is a great thing to do right before you take it. The same principle applies to all competitive athletes, entertainers, celebrity chefs, and everyone else who spends a lifetime trying to perfect a skill they perform in front of a crowd. They think about what they want to happen rather than what they don't, because they know that actions follow thoughts.

If you'd like to test this yourself, find the nearest two year old, hand them a glass of water, and say, "Don't spill that." When they spill it, don't blame them, blame yourself. They did what you told them to do. In order for our brain to understand a command like "Don't spill that," we first have to picture spilling it. The only way we can understand what we're not supposed to do is to picture doing it. The next time you tell someone not to do something, you're instructing them to visualize doing it.

The same thing happens when we tell ourselves not to do something. Like this:

*Do not think of a purple rhinoceros.*

Next time you have to do something challenging, you can think about what could go wrong, and imagine that, or you can think about what could go right, and imagine that. Your choice.

This question might help:

## What if it does goes right?

When you imagine that, try this follow-up question:

## How would it feel if it goes right?

If you're like most people, you've spent a great deal of your life wondering what could go wrong. Why not spend the rest of your life imagining what could go right?

# 17

# What have I overlooked?

When I was a kid I loved to play basketball. I would spend hours dribbling, shooting, driving to the basket, and playing one-on-one with anyone who showed up at the playground. I could beat most of my friends, so I thought I was pretty good. Later, when I tried to play on a team, something curious happened: I was terrible.

My skills hadn't disappeared, but someone would always come out of nowhere and steal the ball. In one-on-one, I'd learned how to play against the person in front of me, but I'd never learned how to pay attention to what was happening around me.

It was a useful lesson in basketball but even more useful off the court. I realized that life is three dimensional, but I'd been playing in only two dimensions.

Think about a problem or challenge you're struggling with. So far, everything you've tried hasn't worked. Ask yourself:

## What have I overlooked?

Listen to what you come up with. Allow your brain to turn over any rock it finds and examine what's underneath. Capture it all. When you're finished, what have you learned?

When you develop the habit of thinking in three dimensions instead of two, you'll have a profound impact on every area of your life.

Consider magicians. They make a living by distracting people. They give you something to pay attention to while they're doing something else. Con men do the same, but with a different motive. So do unscrupulous politicians. They tell you to pay attention to some shiny object, while they're busy doing what they don't want you to see.

We even do this to ourselves. If you find yourself in a situation where something just doesn't feel right, pause for a moment, take a deep breath to center your thinking, and ask:

## What am I missing?

Your answers may surprise you. Our subconscious is often aware of what our conscious mind is not, but we may ignore it if we're distracted by what we think we know, without considering what we don't.

Here's a useful follow-up question:

## What haven't I thought about?

And this:

## What don't I know about this that I should know?

When you ask these questions, and pay attention to your answers, you may discover there's a lot more going on around you than you realized.

# 18

# What can I do differently tomorrow?

*H*ave you ever noticed that ships are steered from the stern? Life works the same way. Tomorrow will take you in the direction you point yourself toward today. The end of each day is an ideal time to look back and ask yourself:

## What would I have done differently today?

Whatever you come up with, ask:

## What can I do differently tomorrow?

Settle on one thing to change. Perhaps it's your attitude, or the way you greet a coworker or your significant other. Maybe it's what you eat, watch, read, wear, or any of the other details that make up your day. Commit to taking that new action tomorrow. Put it on your calendar.

Tomorrow, at the end of the day, ask yourself:

## What did I do differently today?

Then ask the obvious follow-up:

## How did that work?

When you're done, start the process over for the next day.

Think of it as an action forecast. It's like a weather forecast, but you can do something about it. Before you go to bed, check your action forecast for what you plan to do differently tomorrow. It will set your feet on the right path before you even get out of bed in the morning.

# 19

## What if I'm wrong?

$\mathcal{M}$ost of us are willing to acknowledge at least a theoretical possibility we could be wrong. But that rarely stops us from insisting we're right.

We're certain we're right about a lot of things. Politics and religion leap to mind, but we don't stop there. The best baseball team, the right way to raise a child, the correct amount of spice to add to chili, and so on. In our heart of hearts we know we're fallible beings, but that doesn't prevent us from acting as if we're infallible. Although we know we've been wrong before, we're positive we're right this time.

Consider something you believe so deeply you're unwilling to consider any possibility you might be wrong. With this absolute certainty in mind, ask yourself:

### How can I prove I'm wrong?

At first, you might not come up with anything. If you're sure you're right, how can you prove yourself wrong? But here's a sobering thought. Whatever you're most certain about, billions of other people disagree with you. They're as convinced you're wrong as you're convinced you're right.

This is a good time to ask yourself:

## What do they know that I don't?

Listen to everything you come up with. Be honest with yourself. Allow yourself to imagine what other people might know that you don't.

Then ask:

## How would I feel if I knew that?

When you're finished, switch gears and get ready for a much tougher challenge. Consider the thing you're absolutely certain about. With that in mind, ask yourself:

## How can I prove myself right?

You already know you're right. The objective here is to prove it to someone else, with the kind of proof that would convince them.

Facts are a good place to start. Without facts, all we have are opinions. There's no proof in that.

Think of facts as independently verifiable information. That means the other party, the person who disagrees with you, is able to verify any facts you provide. If they can't verify a piece of information you provide, then it's not a fact; it's just your opinion.

Go ahead: prove yourself right. Jot down the facts you'd use to persuade someone else. Take as much time as you need. Remember, facts are independently verifiable by the person you're trying to persuade.

When you're finished, you may find yourself long on opinions and short on facts. Don't be surprised. The more certain we are about something, the less likely we are to rely on facts.

Certainty is based on faith rather than facts. Not faith in the religious sense, but in the sense we don't need facts to feel certain.

Quite the opposite. Facts have a nasty habit of challenging certainty, and certainty doesn't like that.

### *The Certainty of Uncertainty*

Fact-based reasoning begins and ends with uncertainty. Facts can't prove certainty because the next facts that come along might disprove it.

That's the scientific method in a nutshell. At best, any scientific fact is a consensus of opinion about what has been proved to that point; it remains a fact only until a new fact comes along and a new consensus is formed. There's no certainty allowed. A scientific fact will remain a fact only until it has been disproved.

Faith-based reasoning is the opposite; it begins and ends with certainty. Faith remains faith as long as people choose to believe it, regardless of facts. Facts are unnecessary, if not downright objectionable, because they can challenge certainty, but they can never prove it.

When science builds a consensus around a fact, not only is the fact open to challenge, it's expected to be challenged. A fact is a fact only as long as it proves to be true. When it proves to be false, it's discarded like yesterday's news.

There's no similar process for faith-based reasoning. Certainty is all that matters. Facts can neither prove faith-based certainty nor disprove it. At best facts are irrelevant to that certainty. At worst, facts make it uncertain.

This puts human beings in a bind. The more certain we are about something, the less likely we are to rely on facts. To put it bluntly, the more certain we are, the more likely we are to be wrong.

Paradoxically, the best way to defend certainty is to allow it to be challenged. Consider again something you believe so deeply you're unwilling to accept any possibility you could be wrong. With that absolute certainty in mind, ask yourself:

## What if I'm wrong?

Listen to your answers, even if you might be afraid of them. Wait for them if need be. Ask and they will come.

Here's an important follow-up question:

## What are the consequences if I'm wrong?

I like this question because it doesn't challenge our certainty. Instead, it invites us to think about the consequences of being wrong. That's powerful medicine because it allows us to contemplate the bigger picture beyond our opinions.

Whatever the consequences for being wrong, you're subject to those consequences even if you believe you're right. Like gravity; it works the same whether you believe in it or not.

As humbling as it may be to consider the possibility of being wrong, in practice it's a source of great personal power. The ability to change our mind in light of new information is not a weakness: it's a strength. Psychologists call it intellectual humility.

I call it common sense, and like most common sense there's nothing common about it. We cling to our opinions like life preservers in a hurricane. Our opinions reflect our point of view, and our point of view is who we are. To change an opinion that matters to us requires us to modify our point of view. Essentially, we have to change who we are.

That's scary, but we've been doing it our entire lives. That's where change happens. Growth comes at the expense of prior opinions. To change our lives, we have to change ourselves, in small ways and sometimes in large ways, each of which requires us to update our point of view. If you want to change your life at the speed of thought, you have to change your point of view.

One way to encourage this is to be open to new information—indeed, to solicit new information. Whenever you feel most certain about something, it's the perfect time to ask:

## What don't I know about this?

Listen to your answers; they have a lot to tell you. Being human, there's a lot more we don't know than we do. Once we acknowledge this, we open ourselves to additional information. We're no longer afraid of it.

Here's another useful question:

## What do I know about this that might be wrong?

Even if you have the soundest judgment, if you have bogus information, you have a problem. There's a big difference between being wrong and being misinformed. When you're misinformed, you can fix it with the right information. But when you're wrong, you're stuck until you change your point of view.

The most satisfying beliefs are the ones we open to challenge. If they can pass that test, then they're worth believing. The most dangerous beliefs are those we refuse to challenge. Even if we think we're right, we can't escape the consequences of being wrong. That's a high price to pay for a closed mind.

---

## 20

# How can I make the best of this?

---

When life gives you lemons, you're supposed to make lemonade. That looks great on paper, but what if the lemons are rotten?

If this happens to you, ask yourself:

## How can I make the best of this?

Listen to your answers, even if you don't feel like listening. What do you have to lose except for the pain?

If something bad has happened to you, your first thoughts might not be printable. But eventually something you didn't expect will occur to you, something that moves you beyond despair and frustration into forward motion. Maybe it won't make everything right, but it will let you salvage what you can.

You might realize you've learned something worth more than the price you had to pay. You might find an unexpected opportunity lurking in the shadows. Or you might laugh out loud at the absurdity of the situation. All of these are better outcomes than feeling sorry for yourself.

There's a variation on this question that might help. When the situation is so bad that all you have left is your sense of humor, ask:

## How can I make the worst of this?

The creativity of the human mind is bottomless. No matter how bad the situation might be, you can always make it worse. If you let yourself imagine how bad things could be, they won't feel quite as bad the way they are.

It's the perfect time to ask:

## If I could make the best of this, what would I do?

All three of the questions above focus on what you can do. That's how you survive misfortune. If you feel helpless, then you are help-less, like a cork bobbing on an endless sea. But if you focus on what you can do in any situation, on what you can control even if every-thing else feels uncontrollable, then regardless of what has happened to you, you're still in the driver's seat.

# Part 3: Magic at Work

# 21

# What are my strengths?

*I*f you wanted to improve a photo to impress someone on social media, would you choose a good one or a bad one?

We face a similar decision when we decide to improve ourselves. Like photos, we get better results if we start with the good rather than the bad.

Suppose you're a successful salesperson, for example. You're great at figuring out what your customers want and helping them get it, but maybe you're not so good at paperwork. As much as your customers love you, your accounting department does not. If you want to improve your performance at your job, it's a much better investment of your time and energy to get better at what you're already good at. No matter how much you improve your paperwork, that will never make you a better salesperson. But if you become a better salesperson, the rest will take care of itself.

Whatever you do to earn a living, ask yourself:

## What are my strengths?

Spend some time on this. Listen to yourself. If it helps, ask the question this way:

## What am I good at?

This isn't for public consumption, so don't worry about bragging. The idea is to identify your strengths so you can improve them. After you've captured some answers, give yourself a moment or two to reflect.

We tend to be good at what we enjoy doing, and vice versa. That's makes this a useful follow-up question:

## What do I enjoy doing at work?

Whatever it is, chances are you're good at it. Getting better will help you improve at your job, and help you enjoy it more. You'll spend more time doing what you like, and you'll get better at other tasks too. Competence is contagious. It's hard to improve in one area without having some of that competence seep into others.

Consider your list of strengths. Rank them. If you need a refresher on how to do that, go back to Chapter 4 of Book I, *"How do I decide?"* When you've identified your #1 strength, ask yourself:

## How can I get better at that?

Treat this like a brainstorming question. Allow your imagination to come up with as many ideas as you can during the next two minutes. Write them down and reflect on what you've got. Some of your ideas might be obvious; others might surprise you.

Whatever you come up with, you're going to go further in your career, and enjoy it more, if you focus on improving what you already do well.

---

22

---

# Where do I see myself in five years?

$\mathcal{T}$o get where you want to be, it helps to know where you're going. If that seems obvious, ask yourself this question:

### Where do I see myself in five years?

Do you have a clear vision in your mind, or is it murky and uncertain?

You are what you think about. If you know where you want to be in five years, then you're halfway there. If you don't, it's never too soon to start thinking.

It may help to work your way up to five years by asking:

### What do I want to accomplish today?

Listen to your answers and capture them. Then ask:

### What do I want to accomplish this week?

Again, listen and capture. Don't worry if some of the same items appear on this list; keep listening.

Then ask:

## What do I want to accomplish this year?

Don't be surprised if some new items come to mind.

When you finish capturing those answers, ask this:

## What do I want to accomplish in five years?

When you have some answers for this, compare them with your answers to the first four questions. Notice how they change with your timeline.

Two factors influence this. One is our sense of possibility. There's only so much we believe we can accomplish today, tomorrow, or next week. But if we give ourselves five years, it feels like the sky's the limit. Unencumbered by the details of daily life, we give ourselves permission to dream.

There's no law that says you have to stop at five years. Ask this question and compare your answers to the others:

## Where do I see myself in ten years?

With ten years to play with, we can accomplish almost anything we can imagine. We can go to med school, run for president, or finally paint the kitchen.

The other factor that changes with the timeline is our sense of what's important. Oddly, we tend to put important objectives farther out on our timeline, allowing them to be shoved aside by the urgent. That's a mistake we'll fix in the next chapter. For now, think of a ten-year timeline as a tool to help you focus on what's most important to do now, without worrying about what's urgent.

## 23

# How can I focus on one thing at a time?

*T*ime management isn't about time; it's about focus. We can't manage time, but we can manage what we do with it. We just have to figure out what's most important to us and focus on that. It's as simple as doing first things first, one at a time.

### *The Myth of Multitasking*

We live in an age of distraction. Between the constant bombardment from texts, alerts, alarms, notifications, phone calls, emails, and addictive media experiences available 24 hours a day, it's a wonder we get anything done. Sometimes we don't. Yet we're so convinced we can surf all this noise without drowning in it, we've invented a myth called multitasking. We've convinced ourselves we can do two things at the same time.

We can't. Multitasking is an illusion. Sure, you can fold the laundry and talk with a friend at the same time, but only one of those is a complex task, and that's the one that gets your attention.

We can't focus successfully on two complex tasks at the same time, no matter how convinced we are that we can. The best we can do is to switch from one task to the other, over and over again, without ever giving our full attention to either. It takes a toll on our productivity in two ways: By wasting time and by sacrificing competence.

Multitasking takes longer than single tasking, and produces inferior results. Psychologists refer to this effect as the "switching cost" of constantly refocusing our cognitive resources from one task to another and back again.

For instance, we may think we can successfully talk on the phone while we reply to a text. Sadly, we can't. All we're doing is bouncing our focus from one task to the other without fully engaging in either.

The switching cost means we do a poorer job on each task than we would if we performed them one at a time. What's more, each task will take longer than it would if we completed them one at a time. We think we're saving time, but we're actually wasting it.

Another example is when we convince ourselves we can scan a social media feed while we're having dinner with our family and somehow pay attention to both. We can't, any more than they can.

Another multitasking illusion—a lethal one—is that we can text and drive at the same time. Graveyards are full of those who've tried, as well as the innocents they took with them when they failed.

Even jugglers know there's no such thing as multitasking. They create the illusion they're doing so, but they know it's only an illusion. They focus on one ball at a time, skillfully shifting their attention from one to the next, knowing that if they lose focus, they all come crashing down.

If you want to get less done in more time, multitask. If you want to get more done in less time, focus.

Start with this question:


## What one thing should I focus on now?

Listen to yourself and capture what you come up with.

You've encountered this question before, but it's always relevant:

## What's the most important thing for me to do right now?

Whatever answer you come up with, that's your First Thing. That's what you work on first.

First Things can change with context. If your child needs a hug, isn't that the most important thing you can do in this moment? But tomorrow, if you have to work late so you can afford to feed your child, that may be the most important thing to do in that moment.

Whatever you focus on, focus on one thing at a time. Distraction is your enemy. The media and apps that constantly distract us are designed to do exactly that. The people who create those apps need your attention to pay their bills. They don't care if you pay yours. Their job is to grab your attention and keep it as long as possible. Your job is to focus on what you think needs to be done first and do it, one task at a time.

Focus is a skill. You can learn it the same way you learn any other skill. Ask yourself:

## How can I learn to focus?

There are plenty of resources that can help: books, seminars, blog posts, online training, and advice from people who already know how to focus. To find these resources, do an internet search with the question above.

Be careful though. The Internet is an amazing tool, but it's also a great way to get distracted.

Here's a useful follow-up question (for you, not for the Internet):

## If I could focus on only one thing at a time, what would it be?

Then ask this:

## If I could focus on only one thing at a time, how would it feel?

Something wonderful happens when you focus. For one thing, when you know you're working on what's most important to you, distractions are easier to ignore because, by definition, they're less important.

Another benefit is you can feel both relaxed and excited at the same time. You feel relaxed because you're no longer paying attention to interruptions. That reduces stress and increases energy. But you can also feel excited because you're free to focus on one thing and do it well—maybe for the first time.

### The Ivy Lee Question

There's a motivational story that's been making the rounds for the last century about an efficiency expert named Ivy Lee. [1] He was summoned by the CEO of one of the world's largest steel companies, who explained, "We already know what we should be doing. If you can show us a way to get more of that done, then I will pay you anything you ask within reason."

Ivy Lee didn't ask for anything. He told the CEO, "Write down the six most important things you have to do tomorrow and rank them in order of their importance. Tomorrow, start with the most important item on your list and focus on it until you're done. Then work your way through the rest of the list in the same manner. Don't worry if you don't finish. You couldn't finish it any other way, and this way you're always focused on what's most important. Have your managers do the same thing. Do that every day for three months. Then send me a check for whatever you think it's worth."

In three months, the story goes, the CEO invited Ivy Lee back to his office and handed him a check for what today would amount to half a million dollars.

You can turn that story into a useful question, what I call the *Ivy Lee Question*:

What are the six most important things I have to do tomorrow?

Create your list and rank the items. If you need a refresher on how to do that, revisit Chapter 4, Book I, *"How do I decide?"*

Tomorrow, work on the item you ranked number one until you

complete it. Then work your way through the rest of the list, one item at a time. Don't try to multitask; that will only slow you down. Don't worry about finishing your list. Ivy Lee was right. You can't finish it any other way, but this way you're always working on what's most important to you and giving it your full attention.

# 24

# How can I improve me?

*W*e can choose to grow in three areas:

1. What we think
2. What we know
3. What we do

Our progress accumulates over time. Any growth we accomplish today gives us that much more to build upon tomorrow.

Here's a way to jumpstart the process:

### How can I improve me?

Listen to your answers and capture them.

When you're done, consider what you've written. Some of the items on your list may be skills you'd like to acquire or subjects you want to learn. Some may be self-criticisms that identify what you think is wrong with you.

Pick an item from your list. With that in mind, ask these questions:

How can I think differently about____?

And this:

How can I learn to be better at ____?

These two questions align with the first two areas of growth mentioned above. Think of them as a theory about how to improve. The next question is about how to put this theory into practice:

What can I do to be a better at ____?

If there's something you'd like to improve about the work you do, or in any other area of your life, take the time to answer these questions. They encapsulate the entire process of change, and serve as a template to help you improve anything about your life that you're willing to commit to. Try them and see.

---

25

---

# How can I reboot myself?

---

inston Churchill was one of the towering political figures of the twentieth century. He was also a brilliant writer who won the Nobel Prize in literature, as well as a painter. And just for the fun of it, he was a bricklayer who worked on projects around his estate. When he was asked why a man of his accomplishments would deign to work with brick and mortar, he said it allowed him to use a different part of his brain.

Why would he want to do that? In the jargon of our century, Churchill had learned how to reboot himself. You can too, with a question like this:

## How can I use a different part of my brain?

What's the first thing that pops into your mind? The second? Capture your ideas and give yourself a moment to reflect on what you come up with. Any surprises?

Choose an item from your list and ask this follow-up question:

### How would it feel to be doing that right now?

That's a soft reboot. It nudges your thinking and feelings in a new direction.

To go all the way, you need a hard reboot. Choose something you enjoy doing that allows you to use a different part of your brain and do it, even if it has nothing to do with the rest of your life. Think of it as a vacation for your mind.

Even a short vacation can make a difference. Set aside fifteen minutes on your calendar. When the time comes, ask yourself:

### How can I take a fifteen-minute vacation right now?

Have fun with this. Try new things. Discover ways to reboot yourself whenever you need to.

You might want to take Churchill's approach a step further. Instead of using a different part of your brain, consider using a different brain. Think of it as a costume party, but for your mind. Allow yourself to think like any persona who can help you reboot.

For example, you might ask:

### How can I think like a painter?

Or this:

### How can I think like a writer?

Or this:

### How can I think like a ____?

If you take a break from your busy schedule to use a different part of your brain, the other parts will still be working, still thinking, still creating, but without the stress of being front and center. Then, when you get back to work, don't be surprised if you have a whole lot more to work with.

# 26

# What's in it for them?

 *W*hatever you do for a living, you interact with various groups of people. They may be your customers, colleagues, employees, partners, employers, or all of the above.

When we want something from one of them, too often we think: "What's in it for me?" If you want to put your career on the fast track, ask a different question:

## What's in it for them?

Think of something you want from someone and ask yourself that question.

When you've finished, ask this follow-up:

## What do they really want from me?

We tend to think we know the answer to this question, even when we don't, so it never hurts to confirm it. Here's one way:

### If I were in their shoes, what would I want from me?

Imagine that. Then take it to the next step and ask them so you can hear it from the horse's mouth. The objective is to find out how you can make it worth their while to give you what you want. That process begins and ends with them, not with you.

Once you have a clear sense of what they want from you, ask yourself:

### How can I help them get what they want?

Any business transaction is an exchange of value. Whatever you offer the other person has to be so valuable to them they're willing to give you what you want. They get to define that value for themselves.

Transactions don't have to involve money. They can involve anything of value, from time, to personal services, to advice, to anything else on which the parties can agree.

Consider something you want from a person at work. Ask yourself:

### What might they want in return?

Then ask:

### How can I give them more than what they want?

Too often businesses try to offer as little value as possible, while disguising it as more valuable than it is. That's backward. Instead of trying to fool people into thinking you're giving them more than what they're paying for, why not actually give them more? If you've ever left a transaction thinking you made out like a bandit, that's probably because you got more than you hoped for. It's a wonderful feeling.

Why not offer the same feeling to the people you do business with? Turn it into a question:

How can I leave them feeling they made out like a bandit?

When we exchange gifts on holidays and special occasions, we often remind ourselves it's more blessed to give than to receive. This translates perfectly to the modern economy. The marketplace rewards value. Whatever your position in that marketplace, as employer or employee, vendor or customer, consultant or client, you'll be rewarded in proportion to the value you provide. Whatever you want from others, you'll get more of it if you focus on giving them more than you receive.

Here's a question that can help you accomplish this in any transaction:

How can I exceed their expectations?

Here's an interesting twist:

How would I feel if they exceeded my expectations?

Think about it, because that's how they'll feel when you exceed theirs.

## 27

## What's a better way to do this?

*P*rocesses and policies may seem to be set in stone, but the people who thrive in today's economy are the ones who refuse to accept that. They innovate. We tend to think of innovation in terms of technology, but we can innovate in everything, from what we do, to how we do it, to how we think about it.

Consider a task you need to complete for work. With that in mind, ask:

### What's a better way to do this?

Listen to your answers, even the ones that seem off the wall. They might be the best. Capture everything.

When you're done, here's a useful follow-up question that takes a slightly different approach:

### What's a different way to do this?

Notice there's no judgment here. You're not trying to think of a better way to do something—just a different way. This may be all it takes to shake loose new ideas, some of which may be even better than your "better" ideas.

Pick one of your two lists and prioritize the items. Consider the #1 item on that list and ask yourself:

How can I improve on it?

Listen to what you have to say. Capture your answers and give yourself a moment to reflect on them.

In this way, you can refine your answers until you come up with an idea that makes so much sense you can't wait to try it.

There's no need to reserve this kind of thinking for only your most important tasks; you can apply it anywhere. I like to tweak my daily workflow with a question like this:

What if I perform the steps in a different order?

And this:

How can I change my workflow to produce a better result?

Tinker, experiment, have fun.

I once finished a recreation room in twice the time it would have taken me if I'd used the proper type of power saw. Since then, before I begin a project I figure out the right tools to use.

This approach works for everything from carpentry to cooking to software. I wrote two books using off-the-shelf word processing software before it occurred to me to ask:

What tools are designed for people who write books?

As a result, I discovered a wonderful piece of software that helps me get more done in less time with better results.

But I'm still using only a fraction of the power of the software, which leads to another question I like to ask:

## What can I learn about this tool that will help me get more out of it?

Were I to hazard a guess, I would estimate that most of us use no more than twenty percent of the features available to us on our cell phones, computers, software, TVs, microwaves, and every other piece of technology in our lives. Whatever you're doing, whatever you're doing it with, odds are you could learn something new about your tools to help you do it better. Little improvements can make a big difference, not only in the results, but in how much you enjoy what you're doing.

Another thing that can help is to change your perspective. Question the bigger picture. Maybe it's not about doing a task better; maybe it's about doing a better task. Here's a question that can help:

## What's a better way to invest my time?

Instead of asking how to do a better job, you could ask:

## What's a better job for me to do?

Or take it to the 30,000-foot level:

## What's a better way for me to earn a living?

You can change jobs without changing employers. You can also change employers without changing jobs. You might as well consider all the possibilities.

You can innovate in any area of your life, from the tiniest details to the most important things you do. You can innovate at work, in relationships, as well as in who you are and who you want to be. It may mean breaking some rules or creating new ones. It may mean changing your perspective so you see problems and opportunities in a new light.

The only thing holding you back is your willingness to move

forward. If you keep doing the same things the same way, you'll get the same results. If you want different results, you're going to have to do something different. Why not better?

---

28

---

## What opportunities am I missing?

*a* while back I was in the Outer Banks photographing ospreys. As I walked along the beach one morning, the sky shimmering in Carolina blue, I wanted to capture a dramatic closeup of an osprey diving into the surf after a fish. I'd already taken a few decent shots, but I'd yet to get close enough for the picture I wanted. The settings on my camera had to be tweaked just right. I glanced at them to make sure I was ready and I heard a splash so loud I jumped. A few yards from where I was standing, a magnificent osprey had slammed into the water. It was already flying away, shaking the sea from its wings, with a fine fish clutched in its talons. The moment was made for National Geographic. But sadly, not for me. I wasn't paying attention. I was on the right beach, at the right time, at the right spot, with the right equipment, but I missed the shot.

Instead of beating myself up, I asked:

### What can I learn from this?

The answer surprised me. In that moment, I realized we're constantly surrounded by opportunities, but we miss many of them

—maybe most of them—because we aren't paying attention. Focus is a good thing, but it's not the only thing. Whatever you're doing, it never hurts to look up, look around, look behind you, and ask:

## What opportunities am I missing?

Give yourself a minute or two to answer this question. Pay attention to what's happening around you. Start with your physical location and then expand to consider your work, and your life. Capture your ideas. Give yourself time to reflect on them.

If it helps, ask this follow up:

## What other opportunities am I missing?

In Chapter 17, Book II, *"What have I overlooked?"* we learned about living life in three dimensions. This is an extension of that. At any moment, the opportunities we're missing can dwarf those we're aware of. It helps to think outside our field of view.

Here's a question along those lines:

## How can I recognize opportunity?

Opportunity reflects context. If you're trapped in a burning building, getting a promotion is not the first thing that comes to mind.

Assuming that's not the case, consider the opportunities you might be missing in each of these contexts:

What opportunities am I missing to learn a new skill?

What opportunities am I missing to meet new people?

What opportunities am I missing for advancement?

What opportunities am I missing to help someone else?

For any of these questions, here's a useful follow-up:

How can I pay better attention to these opportunities?

We're constantly surrounded by opportunities, only some of which we're aware of. When we broaden our awareness we can dramatically expand our opportunities.

We can even transform it into a useful question, and make it a habit to ask:

How can I become more aware of opportunity?

# 29

# What have I got to win?

*H*ave you ever heard yourself say, *"What have I got to lose?"* As a motivational trick, it's one way to persuade yourself to throw caution to the wind and plunge ahead. But as a question it takes your brain in the opposite direction of where you want to go.

Better to ask:

## What have I got to win?

When we're faced with a heavy lift, it helps to remind ourselves of the payoff. That's when our brain is at its creative best. Here's a question that can help:

## What does winning look like?

There's no difference between winning and losing if you're not keeping score. If you don't know what winning looks like, how do you know you haven't already won?

Here's a useful follow up:

## How will winning feel?

Allow yourself to wallow in the prospect of success. If winning is worth it, then remind yourself of that. By staying focused on what can go right, you motivate yourself to complete the job.

# Part 4: The Magic of People

# 30

---

## How can I be a better listener?

---

*L*istening is at the heart of how we relate to other human beings. Whatever we do in life that involves people, it begins and ends with listening. If you never thought of it that way, it's not too late to start.

As you rethink listening, consider how you might improve your knowledge of the subject.

### How can I learn to be a better listener?

Listening is the most important skill I never learned in school. Your experience may be different than mine, but I never had a course in listening at any level of my formal education.

Fortunately, there are many informal resources to improve listening skills, from books to seminars to online training. You can discover them by doing an Internet search with the question above.

While you're learning about listening, ask:

## What can I do to be a better listener?

Start by listening to yourself. Capture your answers and reflect on them.

Here's a question that can help:

## How do I feel when someone really listens to me?

If you've been lucky enough to experience what it feels like to have someone truly listen to what you have to say, then you understand how important that is to a relationship. You also understand something important you can bring to any relationship:

## How can I help others feel that way?

When I was in high school, a few of us were invited to participate in a PBS TV show being filmed nearby. We arrived at the studio and the crew positioned us in pairs in front of the cameras. They gave each pair a topic to discuss and told us to obey this rule: Before you reply to the other person, repeat what they've said to you—to their satisfaction.

Under the hot lights, with the cameras rolling, my partner began to speak. At first, all I could think about was how to come up with a compelling response. Then I realized I had to repeat what she was saying, to her satisfaction, before I could reply. To make sure we played by that rule, one of the crew sat near each pair to act as a referee.

So I tried to listen, really listen, maybe for the first time in my life. My brain didn't want to do that. I was so busy trying to figure out what I wanted to say it was hard to process what my partner was saying.

She was struggling with the same challenge. In a few minutes we were laughing, partly from embarrassment and partly because the process was scrambling our brains.

I gave up trying to figure out what I wanted to say and simply listened. She did the same when it was my turn to speak. By the end of the exercise, we actually understood one another. Weird, huh?

If you want to bring similar magic into a conversation, then before you respond to what the other person has told you, ask yourself:

## What did they just say?

See if you can repeat it in your mind. If you're worried how that might come across, pause for a moment and act like you're really thinking about what they said, because you are.

It'll take some getting used to, but you can practice it while you're watching TV, or listening to a podcast or the radio. When someone completes a thought, see if you can repeat what they just said.

A word of caution here, don't practice this while you're driving. If you make the effort to really listen to what someone else is saying, your full attention will be on them instead of on the road.

When you practice this in real time with a real person, don't worry about losing your train of thought. You'll follow the conversation better than you normally do, and your words will have more impact than they normally do.

# 31

# Who can help me?

$\mathcal{W}$hatever you want to accomplish in your career, whatever changes you want to make in your life, someone else can help. Maybe all you need is a sounding board. Maybe you'd like them to play a more active role by introducing you to key people, coaching you, or providing financial backing. Whatever you need, someone else can help you get it.

Think of something you want to make happen in your life. With that in mind, ask yourself this question:

## Who can help me?

This is where imagination comes in. When we think of asking someone for help, we tend to think of the people around us. However, they might not be who we need. The best person to ask for help is someone who has already done what you hope to do. If you want to learn how to play a musical instrument, it won't do much good to ask for help from someone who's tone deaf. If you want to become an investment banker, you won't get far by asking a web designer. If you want a promotion, it wouldn't make sense to ask someone who was recently fired from your company.

Here's a way to identify people who can help you:

## Who has done what I want to do?

You don't have to know someone to ask them for help. In my family, there's a recent college graduate who wants to be a sportswriter. He decided to ask for help from broadcasters with the professional teams in his city, even though he didn't know any of those folks personally. Immediately, one of the TV broadcasters replied and asked for a resume so he could show it around. The baseball team he broadcasted had just won the World Series.

When I heard that story, I was delighted with the result. But I was positively blown away with the initiative shown by someone fresh out of school who decided to reach out to those at the top of his chosen profession, people he didn't know, and ask for a helping hand. I wasn't at all surprised that someone offered to help him. People are like that, even successful ones.

When you've determined who can help you, figure out what to ask them for. Here's a good place to start:

## What do I want that person to do?

If you don't know what you want someone to do for you, how can they do it?

Here's a variation on this theme:

## What do I want from them?

When you know whom to ask for help, and what to ask for, there's one more duck to get in a row:

## How can I make it worth their while?

Some people will help you out of the goodness of their heart, like that broadcaster. Others will expect you to sweeten the deal. Here's a question that can help:

### What can I offer them that would inspire them to help me?

When we think of transacting business with someone else, we often default to money changing hands. That's one way to do it. But money is only one of the things that people value.

Imagine there's a successful couple you know who could offer you advice, connections, or maybe invest in a business idea you have. You probably don't have enough money to make it worth their while, so find something else they value:

### What do they need that I can provide?

Suppose that same couple has three kids and constantly struggles to find responsible babysitters. For parents in that situation, a good babysitter is worth more than money. Imagine how grateful they would be if you offered to babysit.

And that's only one of the services you might provide. Maybe they need someone to watch their house when they go on vacation, or someone to bake cookies for the bake sale at their children's school. Maybe they need their house painted. Or maybe they need advice about something you're particularly well versed in. Remember, you're an expert in whatever you know well. You might have the very expertise those folks are looking for.

There are so many creative ways we can help other people get what they want from life. Not only does it feel good to do that, it inclines them to help us.

# 32

# Who can I help?

*N*ews headlines tend to focus on the dark side of human nature. There's no better clickbait than a good murder, war, or scandal. But human beings have a better side. The same DNA that programs us toward jealousy and violence also programs us toward love and service to our fellow human beings.

Whatever the news might say, people like to help people. It feels good. It makes the world a better place. It feeds something in our psyche that can't be fed in any other way. It may not make a good headline, but it makes a good life.

The challenge is that we live in a world full of need. To survive in it emotionally, we may create a layer of indifference to the needs of others; there are so many of them, and only one of us. But there's another way. We can embrace the belief that helping even one person helps us all.

Here's a good place to begin:

## Who can I help?

Listen to what you have to say. Don't judge or dismiss any ideas. Write them all down.

When you have a list, ask the question in a different way:

## Who needs me?

Listen, capture, and reflect.

When you're finished, choose someone from either list. With this person in mind, ask:

## How can I help them?

Think of it as a brainstorming question. Don't be surprised if you come up with some unexpected answers. Listen to what you have to say and capture it all.

With the same person in mind, ask this:

## What do they need?

This may seem like the same question, but it's profoundly different. Too often, when we see someone we could help, we think we know what they need, but that's only from our point of view. We'll be more helpful if we consider the question from theirs. When in doubt, ask them. You might be surprised at how little they need, and how much it can help.

Once you have a sense of what they need, from their point of view, ask yourself:

## How can I help that person right now?

Those last two words are important. Good intentions are nice, but action is what makes the difference.

Here's a useful variation on that question:

## How can I make a positive difference in that person's life right now?

Whatever we choose to do, for whomever we choose to do it, we always get more than we give. Helping other people is the most selfish thing we can do, but it's the best kind of selfish there is.

To help others, you don't have to sell all your belongings and give the proceeds to charity. All you have to do is make it a habit to help at least one person every day. Practice until it becomes second nature.

Here's a great way to start the day:

## Who can I help today?

You don't have to do something dramatic to make a difference in another person's life. You could hold the door for someone struggling with packages. You could truly listen to someone, without judgment or advice. Just listen. You could keep some small bills in your wallet in case you encounter someone who needs those few dollars more than you do, or to put in the tip jar at your favorite carry out. You could allow another driver to cut in front of you, or let a fellow shopper go ahead of you at the checkout counter. You could carve out a small part of your week or month or day to volunteer. The point is: you don't have to scour the globe to find people to help. You can help the person right in front of you.

The same applies at work. Everyone can use a helping hand; why not yours? If you want to stand out in your job, help someone else do theirs. Maybe you could help with a project or serve as a mentor. Maybe you could volunteer to do something that's not part of your job description.

In many cases, what a person needs most is kindness. That requires so little of us, yet it means so much. Imagine a time when you were in a moment of crisis and a stranger showed you a random act of kindness. If that's never happened to you, imagine how you would feel if it did.

Ask yourself:

## Who can I be kind to today?

And this:

## What kindness can I show that person?

When I'm most stressed, one thing that never fails to make me feel better is to smile a genuine smile at someone, or say a heartfelt thank you, or pay attention to another human being as if in that moment they're the most important person on the planet. In that moment, they are.

In a world that often feels like it's coming apart at the seams, kindness is the magic that can hold it all together.

## 33

---

## Who are the most important
## people in the world to me?

---

*A*sk yourself the question above and capture your answers. When you're done, look at the list you've come up with. Are there any surprises?

For most people, this doesn't seem like a hard question to answer. They reel off a list of their closest family and friends. Maybe their dog. But as with other questions, this one suggests follow-ups that might be harder to answer.

Consider one of the most important people in your life. With that person in mind, ask:

### What have I done for them lately?

Don't focus on the things that come with the territory, such as the rituals of a relationship or the requirements of familial duty. They're expected of you, in the same way you expect them from others. Don't get me wrong; it's nice to pay the mortgage, cook dinner, take out the garbage, give birthday cards, and show up for special occasions. But those are givens; you don't get extra credit for them.

Think about the little things, the considerate things, the actions that show you care. With the same person in mind, ask yourself:

What have I done for them lately just because I care?

This might be a short list, so here's a question to make it longer:

What can I do for them right now, just because I care?

These are brainstorming questions, so allow yourself to be creative. Come up with actions that have no reason or occasion to justify them, like bringing them coffee, or flowers, or a book they might like, or giving them a hug—not because it's a special occasion, but because they're special to you.

After you've come up with a few top-of-mind ideas, consider the unexpected.

What wouldn't I normally do for them?

Be as creative as you want. The unexpected often has the greatest impact.

You might also ask this:

What do I wish they'd do for me?

If there's something you would appreciate from them, they might appreciate the same from you.

As with any form of giving, you benefit too. When you get in the habit of doing thoughtful things for others, you'll almost feel guilty because you enjoy it so much. What a great problem to have.

Here's another useful question. With the same person in mind from above, ask:

## How can I enrich that person's life?

Enrichment doesn't have to be about money. It can be anything that improves the quality of life in some way, large or small.

### *Time*

The ultimate gift we can give others is our time. In an increasingly busy world, we often organize our lives to be the opposite of what they should be. Whoever is most important in your life, chances are you spend less time with them than you do with people who are less important to you, like the people at work. Sure, those people matter too, and your job puts bread on the table. But for what purpose? If you're convinced that everything you do at work is for those you love, then you're hallucinating. There's nothing more important you can do for the most important people in your life than to spend time with them.

Turn it into a question and see for yourself. Think of someone who is important to you and ask:

## How can I spend more time with them?

Listen to whatever pops into your mind and reflect on it.

Here's a question that comes at it from another direction:

## What don't I normally do with them?

You know your routine, but what about theirs? What are some of the things they do that don't typically include you? Making dinner? Mowing the lawn? Helping with homework? Watching a ball game? Caring for elderly parents? Taking out the garbage? The most important people in your life are every bit as busy as you are. Imagine if you were busy together.

Consider an activity they do that you don't, and ask yourself:

## What if I joined them?

You can help them or just hang out. Either way, you're doing what they think is important because you think they're important. What a wonderful change of pace.

After you've asked and answered these *Magic Questions* for yourself, revisit the title question for this chapter. It turns out there's a foolproof way to identify the most important people in your life—they're the ones you make time for.

## 34

# How can I improve this relationship?

*H*ave you ever had a relationship where all you could think about was how the other person could improve? As tempting as it is to focus on changing someone else, the only person you can change is you.

Here's a good way to begin:

## How can I improve this relationship?

Listen to yourself and capture everything. Consider what you come up with.

If any of your answers are about how the other person should change, think of them as a hint about what you can change. Our comments about others are often comments about ourselves.

For instance, if you think the other person should be a better listener, ask yourself:

## How can I be a better listener?

If you think the other person should be more thoughtful, ask:

## How can I be more thoughtful?

If you think the other person should take better care of themself, ask:

## How can I take better care of myself?

The new and improved you that emerges from this process will bring something different to the relationship. That's the only way you can improve it.

When you change yourself, you change the dynamic of the relationship. You give the other person something different to respond to, and they may begin to change toward you.

Think of it as breaking a habit. Have you ever had a conversation that feels like you're reading a script? In relationships, especially long-term relationships, both parties tend to respond out of habit. If that produces the desired result for everyone involved, more power to you. But if you want more from the relationship than reciting a script, you need to change your half of the script. You need to change your habitual behavior toward the other person. That gives them an opening to change their habitual behavior toward you.

Even small changes can ripple outward to set in motion big improvements. For example, if you always argue with the same person about a recurring topic, what if you didn't argue? Better yet, what if you asked them how you might think differently about it? That changes the dynamic instantly and puts both of you in problem-solving mode. You might get an earful about how you should change, but don't be surprised if they volunteer something they should change, as well.

Whatever changes you decide to make in yourself to improve a relationship, practice them until they become habits. Consider the examples above. If it feels like an unnatural act to be a better listener, to be more thoughtful, or to take better care of yourself, with enough practice these can feel like the most natural things in the world.

When you commit to changing something about yourself to improve a relationship, these questions can help:

How can I be better at that?

How will I know if I'm better at that?

What would it feel like to be better at that?

Keep in mind that when you change your behavior to improve a relationship, you're not trying to become the person someone else wants you to be; you're becoming the person you want to be. The kind of person you would enjoy relating to. The kind of person you would appreciate as a human being. Do that, and your relationships will take care of themselves.

# 35

# If I were that person, how would I feel?

When we struggle in a relationship, it may be because we can't understand where the other person is coming from. It begs an interesting question:

## What's their point of view?

It's a clever saying, but we can't actually walk a mile in someone else's shoes. Nevertheless, we can make the effort to understand where they're coming from.

Consider a relationship you're having trouble with. Ask yourself:

## If I were that person, how would I feel?

Listen to yourself. Try to imagine what life would be like from the other person's point of view.

When we change our point of view, we change our experience of the world. Not only can it work magic in a relationship, but it's one of the greatest gifts we can give ourselves. Emperor Charlemagne is reputed to have said, "To have another language is to possess a second soul." That's how I feel about exploring another point of view.

Here's a question that can help you begin to understand how someone else sees the world:

If I were that person, how would I want to be treated?

Or this:

If I were coming from where they are, how would I want to be treated?

If this sounds suspiciously like the Golden Rule, it's the same principle, one that's found in all the world's great religions. You can even turn the Golden Rule into a *Magic Question*:

How can I do unto others as I would have them do unto me?

The challenge is to approach this from the other person's point of view, rather than your own:

If I were that person, what would I want?

If I were that person, what would I need?

If I were that person, how would I feel?

If I were that person, what would I want me to do?

Often, when we're struggling in a relationship, we don't understand why the other person is doing what they're doing. That's a good time to ask:

> If I were that person, what would I do?

Or this:

> If I were that person, how would I act?

Here's a different approach:

> What am I missing that they aren't?

And this:

> What are they experiencing that I'm not?

And this:

> What are they feeling that I'm not?

You don't have to ask all of these questions in every relationship, but if you try them at one time or another, you'll have a better sense of which to use in a given situation.

Here are two questions that get to the heart of any relationship:

> How does this person want to be treated?

And this:

> How does this person want to be understood?

If it seems like a lot of effort to understand the other person, imagine how you would feel if the other person made a similar effort to understand you.

The Golden Rule inspires us to treat others as we would have them treat us. But that's not the whole answer. We're all different. We don't necessarily want the same things or want to be treated the same way. The real breakthrough comes from answering this question:

How does this person want to be treated from their point of view, rather than mine?

## 36

## What's really going on?

*C*ommunication is hard because we spend our lives jumping to conclusions. If your significant other came home with lipstick on their cheek, what would you assume?

Your answer says more about you than it does about them.

Through eons, human beings have evolved mental shortcuts that allow us to process more information than we could otherwise handle. These shortcuts include a tendency to *distort* our perception of reality, *delete* information that doesn't conform to our model of the world, and *generalize* our knowledge of one thing to everything else we've lumped into the same category. These shortcuts allow us to make assumptions and reach conclusions that save us considerable time and effort in processing the enormous complexity of our environment.

Unfortunately, we often jump to the wrong conclusions. We generalize, distort, and delete our way to assumptions that make sense from our point of view. In the process, we try to relate to people who generalize, distort, and delete their way to assumptions that make sense from their point of view. It's a wonder any of us ever understands anyone else.

For instance, in a convenience store suppose we see a teenager slip a candy bar into his pocket. We may distort the truth and assume he's a thief because we didn't see him pay for it while we weren't watching. We listen to a news broadcast and unconsciously delete information that might contradict what we believe. We tune in to a political convention on TV, and in a heartbeat, we generalize about thousands of people.

Consider something as simple as a ballgame. When it's over, one side has won and the other has lost. One side is elated. The other is disappointed—perhaps angry. If an official made a controversial call, one side saw it as appropriate, while the other was convinced it was criminally stupid. Both sides witnessed the same game, the same plays, and the same score, but their experience of the event is profoundly different. What really happened? It all depends on their point of view.

All relationships consist of people who delete, distort, and generalize their way to what are often the wrong conclusions, so they can relate to others who are doing the same thing. If you find yourself struggling in a relationship, it helps to keep that in mind. You might even cut the two of you some slack by asking more useful questions.

For example, imagine that one day at work your boss asks you when you'll complete the project you've been assigned. You feel badgered and come up with a snarky response. This is a good time to ask yourself:

## What's going on with me?

Maybe you're having a bad day. Maybe you're dealing with personal problems. Maybe you misunderstood your boss's intent. To clarify, you might ask yourself:

## What conclusion did I jump to?

Or this:

## What assumption did I make?

You might try to recover deleted information:

## What am I missing here?

You might try to unravel distortion:

## What's a more helpful explanation?

These are questions that can help you understand what you may have deleted, distorted or generalized into a toxic assumption. For instance, you may be overly sensitive to what you think of as micromanaging because you've generalized all questions from bosses into the category of badgering. But this boss might want nothing more than to answer a question they've been asked by their boss, a question only you can answer. Or you might have forgotten—in other words, you might have deleted from your thinking—that you had an agreement with your boss to provide a status report today. Or you might have distorted your boss's request into a general displeasure with your work when, from their point of view, it was no such thing.

When you have a clearer sense of where you're coming from, and more constructive alternatives of where your boss might be coming from, you can ask yourself:

## What do I really want to say here?

Or this:

## What do I really want to do here?

The idea is to think these things through before you say something stupid or do something worse. But if you do it anyway, it never hurts to offer a suitable apology, and start the conversation over from a better place—a more informed place.

In any conversation or relationship, feel free to rediscover information your brain has deleted, distorted, and generalized:

What do I really want here?

What am I really after here?

What am I trying to accomplish here?

What's motivating me here?

For extra credit, ask yourself each of these questions about the other person. Your answers will be assumptions, but making the effort to understand where they're coming from can help you right the relationship before it goes wrong.

Here's one of the most useful questions for gaining insight into what's really going on in a relationship:

How would I react to me?

If you wouldn't react well to what you're saying and doing, that gives a sense of why the other person might not.

When you're struggling to relate to someone, here are some questions that can help you take a quick inventory of what's really going on:

What am I thinking that isn't useful here?

What am I feeling that isn't useful here?

What am I doing that isn't useful here?

Whatever you're thinking, feeling, or doing, if it's not helping the relationship, try another approach.

Ask yourself:

What can I do differently here?

The first step in any relationship is to understand where you're coming from. From there, you can do your best to understand where the other person is coming from. The quality of the relationship will boil down to how each of you perceives what's really going on. The bigger the gap between your perception of reality and theirs, the more likely your relationship is headed in the wrong direction. *Magic Questions* can help you turn it around.

---

37

---

## How can I find common ground?

We're programmed by our DNA to notice exceptions. Imagine being an ancient human crossing the African savanna two million years ago. The grasslands stretch before you in every direction as far as the eye can see, but the moment something moves, your attention is drawn to it like a searchlight. Maybe it's a predator, or maybe it's prey. Either way, you have a better chance of surviving until tomorrow if you see it before it sees you.

Consider how this instinct translates into modern life. When we're kids, the first thing we're likely to notice about others is what's different about them, and that's the first thing they're likely to notice about us. No wonder conformity is such a strong impulse for children.

As adults, when we walk into a conference room surrounded by chairs we notice the one chair pulled away from the table. When we have a performance review that is 99% positive we remember the 1% that isn't. Even the cliché that "opposites attract" demonstrates how devoted we are to exceptions. What draws two people together is what they have in common, but when we see them together, we notice how they're different.

When we have a disagreement or conflict with others, our

instinct is to focus on our differences. Think how much harder that makes it for us to find common ground.

We can't reprogram our DNA, but we can reprogram our habits. The human intellect can choose to override the human genome.

We can start by asking a useful question. Consider someone with whom you have a disagreement. With that person in mind, ask yourself:

## What do we have in common?

The answers might not leap out at you. When we're at odds with someone, it can be hard to admit that we have anything in common. But we do—far more than what makes us different, if we only look for it. Give yourself at least a couple of minutes to consider that.

When you're finished, ask this follow-up question:

## What else do we have in common?

Make it a habit to find common ground. If you practice it with everyone you meet, you'll start to notice a difference in how you relate to other people, and they you. For one thing, you'll have more to talk about. There's no better conversation starter than to discuss what you have in common. With practice, you'll begin to realize how much you have in common with everyone you meet, including those you disagree with. You may even find it harder to disagree with them, and they with you. Not because your differences disappear, but because you're not focusing only on your differences anymore; you're also focusing on what you have in common.

When you meet someone, or you're trying to get to know someone better, make it a point to look for areas of shared experience:

What do we have in common about our backgrounds?

What do we have in common about our families?

What do we have in common about how we approach work?

What do we have in common about how we approach life?

What do we have in common about where we grew up?

What do we have in common about our education?

What do we have in common about ____? (music, food, entertainment, hobbies, etc.)

Here are two questions that can help you navigate even the most irreconcilable of differences:

What values do we have in common?

And this:

What beliefs do we have in common?

When you start looking for what you have in common with others, you'll find new ways to move difficult conversations forward. For one thing, when you know you share some interests and background, you'll tend to take it easier on the other person. For another, you'll have a jumping-off place for whatever disagreement you're trying to resolve. If you discover something you have in common, then maybe you aren't as far apart as you thought.

When you disagree with someone, you already have something in common: you disagree. With this in mind, consider what you disagree about and ask yourself:

## What do we have in common about that?

Looking for common ground does the most good where we least expect to find it.

Consider two of the most controversial topics: Religion and politics. If we disagree with someone about religion, we may yet have some beliefs in common. Perhaps both of us believe in God, or disbelieve. Maybe both of us believe in free will. Maybe both of us believe in the right of the other to believe whatever they choose.

That's the common ground at the heart of American politics. The only way I can guarantee my freedom is to guarantee yours, and vice versa. Why not celebrate that? Why not make it the starting point for all our religious and political discussions?

Imagine if we began every such conversation with this question:

## What do we agree on?

The most profound disagreements don't seem insurmountable when we establish common ground. Differences don't feel so different when we realize what we have in common.

Something amazing happens when you build a relationship on common ground: Respect. The more we realize we have in common with someone else, the more we tend to respect that person. If you had the choice of dealing with someone who showed you respect or someone who didn't, which would you choose?

Imagine a relationship built on a bedrock of respect and common ground. Then imagine all your relationships are like that. You can make it happen if you make it a habit to look for common ground.

---

## 38

## Is it worth it?

---

*W*hen we buy something—a phone, a TV, a car—we have an idea if it's worth the price. But what about the choices we make elsewhere in life, the ones we can't evaluate in dollars and cents? Like with people.

From time to time in a relationship, we get locked into a course of action that we feel compelled to pursue, regardless of the consequences. Maybe we're angry, or trying to win an argument, or fighting a political battle at work. If you're in a situation like that, do yourself a favor and ask:

### Is what I'm doing worth it?

Some battles are not worth winning. Is it worth losing a friendship to prove yourself right? Is it worth hurting a loved one because you're angry? Is it worth putting your job at risk to insist on doing things your way?

Whatever the circumstances, you can gain much-needed perspective when you pause long enough to ask:

## What are the consequences of doing this?

Behavior has consequences. In the heat of the moment, we don't always think about that, but we should. We would do well to ask ourselves point-blank:

## Is what I'm doing helping this relationship?

If not, ask this follow-up question:

## What is a better way to proceed?

Even in the heat of battle, you can make a different choice—a more thoughtful choice. If you change your behavior, you change the consequences.

This question can help:

## What can I do that will produce the results I want?

If what you're doing isn't worth it, choose what is.

---

## 39

## Who inspires me?

---

$\mathcal{T}$he ancient greeks advised us to "Know thyself."[1] One of the most useful ways to know who you are is to consider the people you admire. They give you insight into who you want to be.

Consider this question:

## Who inspires me?

Listen to what you have to say. The names you come up with don't have to be famous. I'm constantly inspired by my family and friends. When you're finished, pause a moment and reflect on the names you've written down.

When we think about people who inspire us, it brings a little of their magic into our heart. For instance, when we think about Mother Theresa, we wonder how it must feel to help people the way she did. When we see a child solving a problem in an inspiring way, we wonder what life looks like from their youthful perspective. When we think about any inspiring leader, performer, writer, artist, activist, or colleague, what we admire about them is often something we'd like to add to our own lives.

Choose someone from the list you created, and ask:

## What inspires me about that person?

How you answer this says more about you than about them. We admire a trait or an achievement in someone else because it strikes a chord in us. A part of who they are touches a part of who we are.

Next, ask yourself:

## How can I bring what I admire about them into my life?

I've never read good writing without wondering how I could improve my own, or listened to a moving speech without wondering how I could speak better, or been inspired by a humanitarian without wondering how I could be a little more human to the people around me. When I began to understand the power of *Magic Questions*, I would think of someone I admired and ask myself:

## What can I learn from them?

You can learn from anyone; why not learn from someone you admire? Ask questions that help you identify people who have something to teach you.

## Who has accomplished what I would like to accomplish in life?

## Who's the kind of person I would like to be?

## Who's the kind of butcher, baker, or candlestick maker, I'd like to be?

Here's a question that seems to be targeted at kids, but is one of the most useful questions I know for adults:

Who do I want to be when I grow up?

When you answer this question, you'll know how to inspire yourself.

# 40

# What else?

Whatever questions you ask yourself, you don't usually get the complete answer on your first attempt. That's why it's so important to ask the world's most powerful follow-up question:

## What else?

These two words can change your life at the speed of thought. Use them, practice them, turn them into a habit.

You can greatly expand your repertoire of "What else?" questions by substituting other key words such as *who, when, where*, and *how*. Put any one of these words in front of "else" and watch what happens.

How else?

Where else?

When else?

Who else?

Here's a hint: There's always something else. You don't know everything. You haven't thought of everything. You never will, so keep thinking.

And keep asking. Use "What else?" questions to come up with more ideas, more choices, and more information. Then, when you think you've exhausted all possibilities, ask this:

What haven't I thought of?

If you think this is a "What else?" question in disguise, you're right. Consider where it can take you. Imagine all you can accomplish with it. Then ask yourself:

What else?

# Epilogue

*P*icasso once said of computers, "But they are useless. They can only give you answers."[1]

He had a point. Questions are more important than answers. Even a random question can trigger nonlinear thinking that leads to insights and ideas you might never discover any other way.

With that in mind I've created a website for random questions. Here's the link:

### *Weekly Magic*™

*www.KeithEllis.com/weekly-magic*

*Weekly Magic* provides a random *Magic Question* every week. There's no spam, no ads, and no charge. Just magic.

Who knows what interesting ideas might spring from encountering a question you weren't expecting? And it's fun. If you ever questioned the *8 Ball* when you were a kid, imagine the *8 Ball* questioning you.

*Weekly Magic* continues the journey of personal empowerment you've begun in this book, but with random questions. Please join us to keep your journey going.

# Footnotes

## Prologue

1. "80 Moments That Shaped the World." British Council. Archived from the original on June 30, 2016. Cited by Wikipedia, https://en.wikipedia.org/wiki/Tim_Berners-Lee#cite_note-43.

## 1. What is a Magic Question?

1. *Disclosing information about the self is intrinsically rewarding,* Diana I. Tamir and Jason P. Mitchell; Proceedings of the National Academy of Sciences of the United States of America, May 22, 2012.
2. Vicki G. Morwitz, Eric Johnson and David Schmittlein, *Journal of Consumer Research,* Vol. 20, No. 1 (June 1993), pp. 46-61, as referenced in *The Science of Selling,* by David Hoffeld, p. 101, TarcherPerigee, NY, 2016.
3. Greenwald, Anthony & G. Carnot, Catherine & Beach, Rebecca & Young, Barbara. (1987). "Increasing Voting Behavior by Asking People If They Expect to Vote." *Journal of Applied Psychology.* 72, 315-318, as referenced in *The Science of Selling,* by David Hoffeld, p. 101, TarcherPerigee, NY, 2016.

## 3. How do I change?

1. Descartes, René, Discourse on the Method of Rightly Conducting One's Reason and of Seeking Truth in the Sciences (1637).
2. Alfred Korzybski, *Science and Sanity. An Introduction to Non-Aristotelian Systems and General Semantics.* (The International Non-Aristotelian Library Pub. Co.,1933) 747-61.
3. Richard Bandler and John Grinder, Reframing: Neuro-Linguistic Programming and the Transformation of Meaning (Moab: Real People Press, 1982)
4. Walter Isaacson; *Einstein: His Life and Universe.* (New York, Simon & Schuster, 2007).

## 7. What if I do know the answer?

1. William Shakespeare, *Measure for Measure,* Act 1 Scene 4.

## 5. How can I change my habits?

1. Addictions are another matter, and beyond the scope of this book. You can't give up an addiction as easily as you can change a habit, but you can decide to do something about it. You can choose to recognize that you have a problem and seek help. When you kick the addiction, you can create new habits that will keep you free and clear.

## 8. What is my opinion?

1. This estimate comes from a Wikipedia piece on religions of the world: https://en. wikipedia.org/wiki/List_of_religions_and_spiritual_traditions
2. You can find this famous Platonic dialogue on the web at: http://www.perseus. tufts.edu/hopper/text?doc=plat.+apol.+38a From Plato in Twelve Volumes, Vol. 1 translated by Harold North Fowler; Introduction by W.R.M. Lamb. Cambridge, MA, Harvard University Press; London, William Heinemann Ltd. 1966.

## 12. How do I learn that?

1. "Careers and Learning: Real Time, All the Time 2017 Global Human Capital Trends," *Deloitte Insights*, February 28, 2017.

## 23. How can I focus on one thing at a time?

1. I've found this referenced in a number of motivational books going back a hundred years, but I first heard the story on a recording by Earl Nightingale.

## 39. Who inspires me?

1. Wikipedia has an interesting article on the sources of this aphorism: https://en. wikipedia.org/wiki/Know_thyself#:~:text=dialogue%20with%20Euthyde-mus.-,By%20Plato,it%20to%20motivate%20his%20dialogues.

## Epilogue

1. "Pablo Picasso: A Composite Interview" by William Fifield, in *The Paris Review*, Summer-Fall, 1964.

# Index of Magic Questions™

What would it feel like to be better at that? 191

# The Magic Worksheet™

## THE MAGIC WORKSHEET™

Write your *Magic Question™* here:

_____

Remember the four magic words that make the most of your question:

### *Ask, Listen, Capture, Reflect*

Capture your answers here:

_____

_____

_____

_____

When you're done, and you've had a chance to reflect on what you've captured, ask a useful follow-up, like this:

### *What else?*

Capture your follow-up answers here:

_____

_____

_____

_____

Made in the USA
Coppell, TX
07 January 2021